THE FACTS ABOUT
OSTEOPOROSIS

DID YOU KNOW?

- Small, fair-skinned people are more at risk for osteoporosis than others.

- Chronic yo-yo dieting can cause osteoporosis.

- As you grow older you should change your diet to help prevent osteoporosis.

- The four major factors in the maintenance of our bone density are hormones, diet, exercise, and life-style.

- A lack of dietary calcium and vitamin D are known causes of osteoporosis.

- Excessive intake of phosphorus increases the amount of calcium you need in your diet.

- Strength training helps prevent osteoporosis in women.

- Most patients do not know that osteoporosis is sapping their bone strength—until it is too late.

Over 25 million Americans are affected by the painful, disabling condition known as osteoporosis. How can you prevent it? From taking diagnostic tests to taking immediate, effective preventive measures, here is the clear, expert guide that tells you all you need to know about osteoporosis—and what *you* can do about it.

D1323507

THE DELL MEDICAL LIBRARY

What You Can Do About
OSTEOPOROSIS

Judith Sachs

Foreword by Lawrence G. Raisz, M.D.

A LYNN SONBERG BOOK

Published by
Dell Publishing
a division of
Bantam Doubleday Dell Publishing Group, Inc.
1540 Broadway
New York, New York 10036

NOTE: Medical science and osteoporosis research are constantly evolving and changing so rapidly that the information contained in this book will certainly be modified, added to, and greatly enhanced over the next decade. In the meantime, however, every effort has been made to include the most current data in this book. The reader should bear in mind that this book is not for the purpose of self-diagnosis or self-treatment and that any and all medical problems should be referred to the expertise of appropriate health-care providers.

ISBN: 0-440-21360-6

Printed in the United States of America

Published simultaneously in Canada

October 1993

10 9 8 7 6 5 4 3 2 1

OPM

CONTENTS

FOREWORD

Osteoporosis has been called "the silent disease" because the patient suffering from it has no idea of the loss of bone mass and strength going on inside her body that ultimately may result in crippling fractures of the spine, hip, and other bones. In fact, it may go unnoticed for years because most patients have no noticeable symptoms until the disease is quite far along.

Osteoporosis might also have been called "the silent disease" many years ago because so little attention was paid to it. Now, as our population grows older and we are more attuned to the *prevention* of disease, osteoporosis has become an important and widely discussed health issue.

There is a great deal of new information about the causes and prevention of bone loss and fracture—most of it rather difficult to assimilate and understand. Newspapers, magazines, television, and radio shows are constantly announcing new discoveries, some of which may be truly relevant and important, many of which are dubious or out-of-date. This is why it is crucial to find a good source of real facts and useful self-help material about osteoporosis.

In this carefully researched book, Judith Sachs has assembled the best information currently available on osteoporosis in a clear and readable form. This book will help you to understand your doctor's recommendations and to talk effectively about how these recommendations fit in with your own life-style. The author has reviewed many articles on bone metabolism as well as on the disease of osteoporosis itself and has consulted with a number of leading experts in the field. The result is a balanced, complete overview that reflects as much consensus as can be achieved in writing about this complex medical subject.

While this book is intended for the lay reader, physicians and other health-care professionals working in the osteoporosis field would benefit greatly from reading it. Though it skillfully dissects and interprets traditional medical information, it also covers many aspects of health that physicians sometimes ignore and includes common-sense precautions about safety in the home as well as a perceptive look into the lesser-known psychological and social factors of the disease.

Only a complete approach to osteoporosis prevention such as offered here can be truly effective in reducing the terrible toll in loss of function, high health-care costs, and increased mortality that results from osteoporotic fractures in our aging population.

It is important to realize that we still have many gaps in our knowledge of osteoporosis. Although this book indicates that there may be a large number of risk factors, we still see patients who develop severe and progressive disease but do not seem to differ in background or medical profile from women with minimal or no disease. We still need to know much more about how the skeleton is built up and broken down. Moreover, we really do not have effective treatment for osteoporosis once it is established —or a safe and effective way of stimulating new bone to form once the disease has taken hold.

Many clinics and laboratories throughout the world are actively engaged in research on the causes, prevention, and treatment of osteoporosis, but much more work is needed. Until new information is available, the guidelines provided here by Ms. Sachs will serve the reader well.

This book will help you to assess your own risk in developing osteoporosis and to work effectively and intelligently with your physician to establish a program that can minimize your risk.

—LAWRENCE G. RAISZ, M.D.
Head, Division of Endocrinology and Metabolism
Osteoporosis Clinic
The School of Medicine of the
University of Connecticut Health Center

ACKNOWLEDGMENTS

I would like to express my thanks to the following individuals for their time, expertise, information, advice, encouragement, and moral support:

Lawrence G. Raisz, M.D., Osteoporosis Center, University of Connecticut Health Center, Farmington, CT

Robert Lindsay, M.D., Helen Hayes Hospital, Regional Bone Center, W. Haverstraw, NY

Diane Meier, M.D., Department of Geriatrics, Mt. Sinai Medical Center, New York, NY

Marc K. Drezner, M.D., Department of Endocrinology, Metabolism and Nutrition, Director of the Sarah W. Stedman Center for Nutritional Studies, Duke University, Durham, NC

Steven Gecha, M.D., Princeton Orthopedic Associates, Princeton, NJ

Maurice Attie, M.D. The late Dr. Attie was Director of the University of Pennsylvania Osteoporosis Clinic when I interviewed him.

Sandra C. Raymond, Executive Director, National Osteoporosis Foundation, Washington, DC

Fred Kaplan, M.D., Department of Endocrinology, University of Pennsylvania, Philadelphia, PA

Guy E. Abraham, M.D., Optimox Corporation, Torrance, CA

Gordon S. Goei, M.D., Beverly Hills, CA

Richard Taylor, M.D., Atlanta, GA

Harinder Grewell, M.D., Torrance, CA

Kirk M. Palmer, Lunar, Madison, WI

Pat Chichon, R.N., Herbalist and nutritionist, Ringoes, NJ

Nicolette Schwartzman, Newtown Acupuncture Associates, Newtown, PA

Laurie G. Lindberg, National Osteoporosis Foundation, Washington, DC

Judith Wortman, National Institutes of Health/National Institute of Arthritis and Musculo-skeletal and Skin Diseases, Bethesda, MD

INTRODUCTION

Over 25 million Americans are currently affected by the painful and disabling condition known as *osteoporosis,* which literally means "porous bones." This disease causes approximately 1.3 million fractures each year in people over 45. If you are approaching midlife or beyond, you are probably concerned about whether or not you will break a vertebra or hip as you grow older. Since this condition attacks one third to one half of all postmenopausal women, and nearly half of all individuals—male and female—over 75, the question is often *when* rather than *if* it will become a problem.

Doctors used to view osteoporosis as an inevitable consequence of aging. Now they know that it is not part of the normal aging process. Many cases, particularly the early onset cases, can be prevented by diet, exercise, medication, and proper monitoring of the process of bone loss.

Taking care of your bones throughout your life, from childhood and adolescence to your reproductive years and on into midlife, can make the difference between an active, vital existence in your later years and one of chronic pain and immobility. Early prevention means lifelong maintenance of your bones. *And the earlier the preven-*

tion, the better your chances of avoiding osteoporosis entirely or managing its problems far better. As a matter of fact, osteoporosis has been described as a disease of the elderly that has its roots in childhood.

The stronger your bones become during your peak years of bone growth—from birth to 35—the stronger your bones will be as you age. If you give yourself the best chance for maximum bone mass and density early on, you may be able to circumvent a disease you are genetically predisposed to—or at least ward it off for 10 to 20 crucial years.

Preventive care means eating a balanced, calcium-rich diet; exercising regularly; and avoiding cigarettes, alcohol, caffeine, soft drinks, and crash diets. It's really an easy, comfortable prescription for good health that can ensure a lively body at 70, 90, or 120—however long you may live.

A century ago, few women lived past menopause, when the female body loses the protective effect of estrogen on bone tissue. Therefore, not that many women had to worry about breaking a hip and being confined to a wheelchair or walker for the rest of their lives. But today, with a woman's life expectancy at 78 and steadily increasing, she has an urgent mission to keep her body in the best condition possible for all those quality years she has ahead of her.

Two different types of osteoporosis will be discussed in this book. The first generally develops in women after menopause, and the second hits both sexes after age 75. The likelihood of developing this disease has a lot to do with life-style—including the way you've managed your diet, exercise, and environment up to now and the way you're going to change those elements to keep your bones in the best shape possible.

This year, more than 300,000 of us will break a hip, 500,000 of us will suffer vertebral fractures, and over 200,000 will break a wrist. All told, osteoporosis diagnosis, treatment, hospitalization, physical therapy, and long-term care costs range from $7 billion to $10 billion annually, and the price is rising. By the year 2020, it will cost us $30 billion annually. Osteoporosis is a major health problem in this country, and it will burden our health-care system even more severely as the population ages.

What can be done? In this book, we'll tell you what medical science currently knows about bone—how it is formed and remodeled throughout the years and how the process slows down and changes as we get older. We'll explain why you might be at risk for osteoporosis and tell you how the disease is diagnosed and what tests can be done to show how much bone mass you actually have. Because the best treatment for osteoporosis is staying well, we'll give you a complete preventive diet and exercise program, along with some easy life-style changes you can make now to help guard against falls and breaks. Then we'll discuss medical treatment of osteoporosis and explain why hormone replacement therapy and supplemental calcium are so helpful. We'll also explore some of the newer treatments currently being investigated.

Finally, we will talk about alternative treatments that deal with both body and mind—flexibility training, physical therapy, psychological adaptation, and techniques for the control of pain.

With the knowledge that you can gain about the amazing processes of your skeletal structure, and the tools at your disposal for maintaining your bones, you will be able to prevent osteoporosis or deal with it effectively during the long life you have ahead.

WHAT IS OSTEOPOROSIS?

Osteoporosis is a chronic disease of bone loss that occurs over time. As the disease progresses, the remaining bone in the skeleton is of good quality, but there's an insufficient quantity of it to support the body's activities. In this chapter, we'll explain what bone is made of, how the process of remodeling bone works, and how the body's unique system of checks and balances fails when osteoporosis strikes.

Bone is a *dynamic* tissue. It is always changing, always in the process of reacting to outside stimuli—chemical ones, such as hormones and enzymes; electrical impulses from the nervous system; and mechanical ones, involving the movements you do and the way in which you do them.

The bones you have today are not the bones you'll have ten years from now. Most bone has a 10 percent yearly turnover, so that the body is always replacing new tissue for old. As we age, however, this turnover, or "remodeling," process doesn't function as well as it should. If old bone is removed but isn't replaced in the same quantity as before, the bones will become progressively weaker. The outside architecture of the house often remains the same, but as the inside structure gets thinner, there just isn't enough of it to support the outer shell. It's at this stage that fractures begin to occur.

THE COMPOSITION OF BONE

Bone is actually two different textures. Inside is *trabecular bone* (also called *cancellous bone*), which has a honeycomblike, spongy consistency, threaded through with marrow, blood vessels, and capillaries. This spongy interior is covered with *cortical bone* (also called *compact bone*), the smooth, firm tissue of the skeleton.

A typical long bone (like a thigh bone) is a shaft made of cortical bone on the outside. It ends in a knob that is filled with trabecular tissue. The cavity running down the center of the bone's shaft is filled with marrow. The outer covering of the bone is a membrane, and its inner layer is thick with cells called *osteoblasts,* which are responsible for bone formation; the lining of the marrow cavity is another membrane that contains *osteoclasts,* bone cells that are responsible for repair and growth.

BONE ON A MICROSCOPIC LEVEL

Within bone tissue, there is a *matrix,* that is, the intercellular material composed of protein threads shot through with nerves and blood vessels, and there is inorganic matter made of *hydroxyapatite.* This mineral substance is mostly a calcium phosphate salt, but it also contains carbonate, fluoride, and magnesium. The outer shell of bone is a hard amalgam of all these minerals arranged in layers.

In order for the constant buildup and breakdown of bone tissue—the process known as *remodeling*—to occur

A typical long bone.

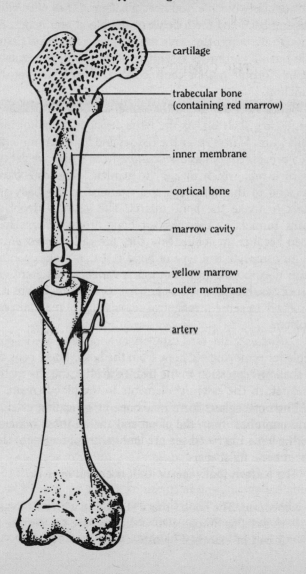

cartilage

trabecular bone
(containing red marrow)

inner membrane

cortical bone

marrow cavity

yellow marrow
outer membrane

artery

throughout your life, you need a balanced flow of calcium passing back and forth between the blood and bones. Although 99 percent of your calcium is in the bone tissue, the final 1 percent is essential to the blood. It regulates blood clotting, muscle contraction, and nerve and muscle function.

Bones start out life in the womb as rods of cartilage, a temporary skeleton. As the fetus develops, bone-forming cells (*osteoblasts*) enter the tissues and lay down minerals in a process known as *ossification,* from which we get the word *ossify,* which means "to harden." The osteoblasts respond to the hormones and vitamins in the body and start to make the bone matrix. The young osteoblasts form tunnels as they deposit bone around themselves, then become immobile. Now they are called *osteocytes.*

An osteocyte is a type of bone cell that makes contact with neighboring cells through a variety of different cell processes. It's not quite clear what its function is, but it is probably to sense mechanical signals and to maintain nutrition.

Osteoclasts, the final category of bone cells, are responsible for removing old bone from the body. These cells dig a shallow depression in the hydroxyapatite and the matrix and return the essential elements to the bloodstream.

Then osteoblasts form new bone by providing calcium and phosphate from the blood and adding these minerals to the bone matrix (made predominantly of collagen) that gives bone its shape.

The pattern that repeats itself over and over is:

Activation. The bone surface is covered with osteoblasts that act as lining cells, which prepare the surface so it can be resorbed by osteoclasts.

Normal remodeling process.

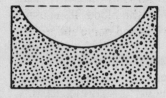 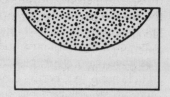

Osteoclast digs out
shallow depression

Osteoblast fills it
in with new bone

Resorption. Osteoclasts come to the remodeling site and, under the influence of various hormones, reproduce themselves. Over a seven- to ten-day period, they form a ruffled border where some of the mineral and matrix is loosened and dissolved.

Reversal. Macrophages (white blood cells that help in the healing process of any injury or illness) appear on the resorbing surface.

Formation. Osteoblasts replace resorbed bone (usually in about three months' time), stimulated by different hormones.

This digging out and filling in goes on throughout childhood, up through adolescence. Your bones grow quickly at this time of life. By the time you're about 15, you've reached your full height, but your bones increase in density for the next 10 or 15 years. You have about 10 percent bone turnover a year, with more formation than resorption. During our twenties and early thirties, the process evens out and works in perfect balance. You're at your peak for bone mass when you're about 30 or 35.

HOW BONES BECOME POROUS

The brilliant equilibrium of the remodeling system begins to get out of balance as we get older. Up to age 35 or so, various hormones have encouraged the laying down of calcium into your bones and have prevented it from being resorbed into your bloodstream. We aren't sure how much bone loss occurs between 35 and 50—it probably depends greatly on factors unique to each individual.

But if you are a woman, your hormonal levels decrease during the perimenopausal years (from about 42 to 50, for most). And at this point, the process begins to reverse itself. Resorption overtakes formation. You start to lose bone mass and mineral content. Your bones lose their ability to hold on to the calcium you consume. The holes in the trabecular honeycomb, which previously resembled a piece of Swiss cheese, widen until this tissue starts to look like a cyclone fence with a lot of broken wires.

Mechanical stress on the body also changes with age. We tend to move less and sit more. Then, too, other disease processes affect our bone mass and density, as do certain medications for other conditions. Over time, the system gets *uncoupled;* that is, the osteoclasts are more active than the osteoblasts and eat away deeper depressions than the osteoblasts can fill. The cortical exterior of bone gets harder and more compact; but inside, the trabeculae are thinning out and often becoming too fragile to support the outer structure. When this occurs, fracture may be imminent.

If the bone tissue becomes too thin, it loses its resilience and breaks easily during a fall or hard knock or when under stress. An action that causes the vertebrae, which have a much greater proportion of trabecular bone than cortical bone, to be jammed together can easily

Normal bone.

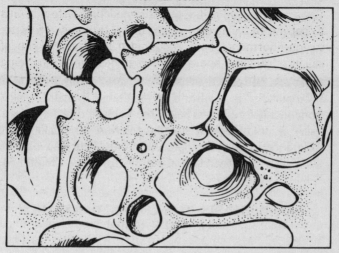

Thinning bone with fractures from advanced osteoporosis.

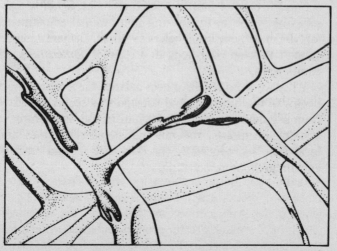

cause a fracture. Some women have broken ribs just by sneezing. The vertebrae can even collapse from the weight of an individual's own body.

Once fractures start (usually when you've lost 30 to 50 percent of your bone mass), the disease has already reached an advanced stage. Although women with fractures can be treated effectively to stop the *progression* of osteoporosis, it is obviously preferable to halt or slow bone loss *before* it gets below the fracture threshold. Diet, exercise, and calcium supplementation can make a big difference in your osteoporosis profile—but you have to start early being vigilant about all three (see Chapter 5).

HOMEOSTASIS: THE CHEMICAL BALANCE OF YOUR BODY

There are thousands, perhaps millions, of influences that act on the cells of your body each moment. Sending messages back and forth, making infinitesimal adjustments for the most exquisite balance—these elements act in concert to keep your body in a state of *homeostasis,* or equilibrium.

When your body falls out of balance for any reason, it begins to malfunction. And osteoporosis seems to derive from a gradual lack of equilibrium in the fine-tuning of systemic hormones, minerals and vitamins, enzymes, and local factors produced by the cells that act and react to encourage bone remodeling.

BONE METABOLISM AND
AVAILABLE MINERALS

One of the chief influences on bone is the balance among, and availability of, the minerals calcium, phosphorus, magnesium, and sodium. We may ingest sufficient amounts of these minerals through the foods we eat and yet not have them readily available to our bones because of poor absorption. These minerals will be discussed in detail in Chapters 5 and 7.

THE ENDOCRINE SYSTEM AND HOW IT
AFFECTS YOUR BONES

Your endocrine system consists of glands that secrete *hormones,* or chemical messengers, that travel through your bloodstream to help regulate many functions in your body. The hormones have special *target tissues* on which they act, and they attach to these tissues via *receptors,* or doors that open into the tissues. The endocrine system includes the following glands: pituitary, thyroid, parathyroids, adrenals, pancreas, and gonads (sex organs—ovaries for women and testes for men).

The various glands produce many hormones that affect a variety of target tissues. For our purposes, however, we'll only discuss those that affect bone.

The *gonads* produce *estrogen* (for women) and *testosterone* (for men). These essential hormones are greatly responsible for osteoclastic activity. For women, the lack of estrogen after menopause is a big factor—many experts believe it is *the* biggest factor—in rapid bone loss at this time of life.

The *adrenals* produce a glucocorticoid hormone known

as *cortisol,* which affects glucose and amino acid metabolism. These hormones work on many tissues, including the bones, the muscles, and the liver. The adrenals also produce some estrogen, and after menopause, this supply of hormonal activity is particularly important to women at risk for osteoporosis. These glands also produce testosterone, which is important to men's bones as they age, just as estrogen is to women's bones.

The *thyroid gland* increases the metabolism of most of the body's cells, thereby stimulating growth and development. It produces *thyroxine,* a hormone that, if produced in excessive quantity, can stimulate too much bone resorption. It can also increase the amount of calcium excreted through the urine. The thyroid produces *calcitonin* as well, which serves to lower the amount of serum calcium (calcium circulating in the blood).

The *parathyroids* are four small glands behind the thyroid gland that are responsible for raising blood calcium. They do this by producing a hormone known as *PTH* (*parathyroid hormone*), which is vital in increasing calcium absorption from bone and enhancing absorption by the kidneys. If there is less PTH produced in the body, this in turn reduces the amount of active vitamin D. In the elderly, there tends to be an increase in PTH activity, which is probably due to lower calcium and vitamin D supply and activation in the bone tissue. But since there is also less osteoblastic activity forming new bone, and a lower level of calcitonin secretion, there is also a higher calcium level in the blood. This means that more bone loss can occur.

These glands also stimulate the conversion of *vitamin D* from its inactive form to its active form. In its active form, it is known as 1,25-dihydroxyvitamin D_3, and it stimulates calcium absorption from the gut. After menopause, the drop in vitamin D levels means less calcium can be absorbed by the gut, and therefore, less calcium will be available to make new bone. This vitamin may also work directly on bone tissue in the course of the remodeling process.

OTHER FACTORS THAT WORK ON BONE

Enzymes are chemical catalysts that must be present in order for certain activities to take place in the body. The *liver* produces enzymes that assist in bone remodeling by making various vitamins and minerals available to the bone cells. *Metabolic enzymes* help with the function, repair, and maintenance of the body's tissues and organs. *Digestive enzymes*—of which liver enzymes are one category—help to break down food into its component parts so that the body can use its nutrients.

Local factors are other hormones that may have significant influences on bone. Among them are prostaglandins, interleukin-1, insulinlike growth factor (IGF-1 and -2), tumor necrosis factor (TNF), and transforming growth factor–beta (TGF–beta). These factors interact with systemic hormones, particularly PTH and 1,25-dihydroxyvitamin D_3.

MULTIPLE INFLUENCES ON BONE REMODELING

So many outside influences affect bone, and the experts really aren't sure exactly how all the elements of this system come together. Anything that tips the balance of your hormone control mechanism—an overabundance of thyroid hormone, an overactive parathyroid gland, too much of the adrenal hormone cortisol, not enough dietary calcium, a prolonged period of bed rest, even a trip on a space shuttle!—will change the remodeling pattern of your bones. And the resultant bone may be considerably weaker, leaving you, in all senses of the phrase, without a leg to stand on.

OTHER DISORDERS OF BONE

Osteoporosis is not the only disease of bone tissue. Other bone diseases occur because of problems with the *quality* rather than the *quantity* of bone produced—as is the case in osteoporosis. If you are having problems with pain or fracture, you and your physician may not know immediately which bone disorder affects you.

Other bone diseases include the following:

- *Paget's disease* is a chronic inflammation of the bones, which makes them soften and thicken. In an advanced stage, this can lead to a deformity where the long bones are bowed inward.

- *Osteomalacia* is also known as "adult rickets." This disorder, where the bones soften in texture, is caused by a lack of usable vitamin D in the body, which prevents bones from hardening or mineralizing well. This, in turn, prevents the absorption of calcium and phosphorus through the intestine.

- *Osteomyelitis* is an inflammation of bone—particularly the marrow—caused by bacteria in the bloodstream that can invade the marrow and the membrane covering the outer layer of bone.

- *Osteoarthritis* is an immune dysfunction where excess calcium in the blood deposits in the joints between bones and cartilage, causing them to become painful and deformed.

- *Multiple myeloma* are tumors that originate in the cells of the bone marrow. This disease is progressive and usually fatal.

- *Osteopenia* simply means a lessened amount of bone tissue, regardless of cause. Osteoporosis, evidently, is one form of osteopenia.

PREVENTION OF OSTEOPOROSIS: A GOAL FOR ALL OF US

The four major factors in the maintenance of our bone density are:

- Hormones

- Diet (including calcium content)

- Exercise

- Life-style

Although many factors may put you in a high-risk category for this disease, there are definite preventive steps you can take that encompass these four factors. All these steps will be outlined in future chapters.

The important thing is to remember that the better we take care of our bones, the more time we'll have to lead an active, vital life. And the more active and vital we are, the better our bones will be. It's a positive cycle that can, in fact, make a big difference in your bone health.

TWO

ARE YOU AT RISK?

How do you really know whether you are a candidate for osteoporosis? There are certain specific factors that may predispose you to this disease. Some you can change; some you can't. Naturally, you are at higher risk, and more likely to contract the disease, the more factors you have. This does not mean, however, that you will *necessarily* develop osteoporosis in later life. You can alter your bone profile significantly by changing the way you eat, exercise, and live.

Knowing that your family background, physical build, and life-style choices might predispose you to osteoporosis gives you the extra impetus to see a physician early on to find out where you stand and what health concerns most affect you. Whether or not you fit into any—or all—of the categories mentioned in this chapter, you cannot be sure that you are at risk unless you are tested. This is why bone densitometry measurements—which detect low bone mass—are essential in preventive treatment (see Chapter 4, "Biochemical and Densitometry Testing").

Seeing a physician and getting tested are the first two vital steps in a preventive health care plan you can maintain throughout your life.

WHAT KINDS OF RISKS ARE THERE?

Some elements—family background, age, sex, and race—are obviously unchangeable. You are handed a certain genetic makeup before you even enter the world, and it's yours for life. Other elements also may be beyond your control: Never having had a child places you at higher risk for osteoporosis than if you'd had one; going through a surgical menopause in your twenties or thirties also puts you at additional risk. Likewise, if you are being treated for a chronic disease with certain drugs that weaken your bones, you have to weigh the alternatives. You can't simply stop taking your medication because you're worried about possibly contracting osteoporosis in the future.

But other elements—what you eat, how you exercise, the life-style decisions you make about alcohol and smoking—these are things over which you have ultimate say. And making positive changes in these categories can affect the rest of your profile.

Let's take a detailed look at all the risk factors to see where you fit in.

Genetic Factors

- Female

- Caucasian or Asian

- Family history of osteoporosis

- Fair complexion

- Small frame

Sex Women are more at risk than men for several reasons. Women are generally smaller and have lighter bones than men. The strength of a bone depends on its total mass rather than on how dense it is. Men start out with about 30 to 40 percent more bone mass, though they only have 10 to 15 percent more density. With less bone mass during the peak years, women start from a weaker position during the aging process, when everyone loses both mass and density.

But women are at a second disadvantage because they go through menopause. Both sexes are dependent on their reproductive hormones (estrogen for women and testosterone for men) to help lay down calcium into new bone and keep it from being resorbed into the bloodstream or excreted in urine or sweat. But only women suffer a drastic drop in their hormones at menopause, when the menstrual cycle slows and eventually stops, and less and less estrogen circulates in their bodies.

Men undergo a slight decrease in testosterone production from their late seventies onward, and certain diseases may decrease the male hormone output, but in general, men's bones are better protected hormonally throughout their lives than women's.

Race Much of the way your bone tissue builds and rebuilds itself has to do with your ethnic background; for example, black women tend to have heavier bones (some Hispanic women have heavier bones, but not all). The protective element of the darker-skinned races' body build was probably a selective adaptive mechanism for our ancestors, although it's not clear why. Although there are black and Hispanic women who develop osteoporosis, the majority retain this genetic protection.

Family History of Osteoporosis Family history is an enormously important factor for several reasons. First, knowing that your mother or grandmother fractured easily when she was older tells you that you have probably inherited her propensity for thinner, more porous bones. It was part of the DNA (deoxyribonucleic acid—the genetic material) handed to you at birth, and you can't alter it. But you *can* alter the outcome. By getting tested early on, by finding out how dense your bone is and how quickly or slowly you are losing bone mass, you can actively make a stab at changing your inheritance. And you will probably have more motivation than women who don't have osteoporosis in their families to take good care of your bones today and in the future.

Fair Complexion, Small Frame People with fair skin and small, light frames are at a genetic disadvantage. No one is certain why fair skin is a risk factor. A small frame means that even at peak bone mass, at about age 35, the density of these bones is less than optimal.

Nutritional Factors

- Thinness

- Always a yo-yo dieter (losing weight, putting it on, taking it off throughout your life)

- Low dietary calcium consumption

- Low vitamin D intake (dietary or directly from sun exposure)

- High caffeine consumption

- High soft drink consumption

What we eat throughout life makes a real difference in our bone health. But unlike genetic factors, nutritional factors can be changed. You can make a positive difference in what you put into your body. Because bones grow slowly, you may have years ahead of you to affect the laying down of stronger, more resilient bone if you eat better.

Thinness   Being thin—the first risk factor on this list—may be simply your build and therefore a genetic factor. But for many women in our society, thinness is an imperative. As it happens, it is better to carry five extra pounds as we get older, and not just for extra padding in case of falls!

Heavier women, who have more and larger fat cells in their bodies, utilize a hormone known as *androstenedione,* an androgen precursor, as extra hormonal protection after menopause. This male sex hormone (testosterone is the more commonly known male counterpart) is present in small amounts in women's ovaries and in the adrenal glands. After menopause, when estrogen levels fall, the androstenedione is converted by the body's fat cells into *estrone,* a less potent form of estrogen. The more fat cells, the more estrone and the more protection for your bones. In addition, heavier women have a built-in weight-bearing advantage because they are carrying around extra pounds that stress the skeleton in beneficial ways.

Yo-yo Dieting   Many women stay thin by repeatedly submitting themselves to the punishment of yo-yo dieting.

Radical changes in the kinds and amounts of food you ingest stress the entire body. When you put yourself on a restrictive diet, your metabolism reacts to prevent starvation. It begins to conserve energy and slows down. Then, when the diet ends, or when the dieter binges, the metabolism speeds up again. Hundreds of hormones and enzymes come into play, and as they are alternately secreted in larger and smaller amounts, they fall out of balance.

Dieters often keep themselves thin by substituting low-cal soft drinks (which contain no calcium at all and are high in phosphates) for foods and beverages that do contain calcium. The acid/alkaline balance of the body is also affected by dieting. Good bone formation depends on the equilibrium of all these elements. Enough crash dieting can upset the balance completely, particularly during the teen years of increased growth.

Soft Drink and Caffeine Consumption It's a good idea to wean yourself—and your children—away from soft drinks and caffeine. Caffeine inhibits the action of bone formation and increases the excretion of calcium through the urine. Soft drinks contain phosphates (as do processed foods), which bind to calcium and make it difficult to metabolize. Then, too, kids who rely on soft drinks to quench their thirst are not drinking milk—the beverage they should be consuming in quantity. Children who just can't stand a plain glass of milk can be encouraged to drink milk shakes, yogurt shakes, and juices. If your child will drink *only* chocolate milk, it's better than having no milk at all. However, the oxalic acid in chocolate binds to the minerals in foods, making it difficult for the body to absorb the calcium in the milk. Adults can switch to skim milk, herbal teas, and juices. Both should consume lots of good, fresh water.

Lack of Dietary Calcium and Vitamin D   We must eat a balanced, high-calcium diet in early life if we want good bones in our later years. The childhood and teen years are when bone growth counts the most. If you currently have young children and/or teenagers, *this is the best time to alter their eating habits* to ensure good bones in the future. If they reach their peak bone years with as much bone mass and density as they can possibly attain, they will be in far better shape as they age.

As we get older, we still need the nutritional benefit of adequate calcium and vitamin D. A sensible diet keeps the body and all its processes in alignment, offering the proper nutrients in the right balance to maintain and repair tissue. Studies have shown that postmenopausal women, who had already lost much of their protective estrogen, still had fewer fractures once they began ingesting more calcium. Those who had a particularly low calcium intake at the beginning of the study (below 400 mg [milligrams] daily) saw the greatest benefit. The National Osteoporosis Foundation recommends 1,000 mg of elemental calcium daily for women past menopause.

The vitamin D we take in makes it possible for our bodies to metabolize calcium. There are a variety of "fortified" products now that include extra vitamin D, but the best source is the sun itself. Just 15 to 20 minutes a day will give you the vitamin D you need. And while you're outside, it's almost impossible not to derive another benefit: Walking, working in the garden, jogging, or biking all fulfill another requirement for good bones—giving them weight-bearing exercise to do!

Life-style Factors

- Cigarette smoking

- Alcohol and recreational drug use

- Physical inactivity

- Childlessness

- Prolonged lactation

- Lack of sodium fluoride in water (possibly—this is still a point of controversy in most scientific circles)

Cigarette Smoking   There's no halfway measure when it comes to cigarettes. Use any plan or method that works for you and just stop smoking. If you've stopped, don't start again. Cigarettes are killers—they attack all parts of the body. Their effect on the lungs is well documented, but they also increase the risk of heart attack, inhibit the brain from getting enough oxygen, and interfere with the formation of new bone tissue. Smokers also tend to go through menopause about five years earlier than they would if they did not smoke, which means less protective estrogen in their systems for more years of life.

Another real reason to stop is that you can be a role model for your kids. Children think it's "cool" to smoke. Until very recently the media have even promoted the image of "happening people" lighting up.

Alcohol and Recreational Drug Use   Alcohol and recreational drugs are also detrimental to bone development and maintenance. The ethanol in alcohol appears to create more porous bones. More than moderate consumption of these addictive substances alter perception and balance and therefore make people more prone to falls, adding to fracture risk.

Alcohol abuse is becoming an increasing problem with adolescents of every social class. Alcohol is generally available in the home, and its use is condoned by parents much more than marijuana or cocaine. But habitual use of any of these drugs can kill; and all are detrimental to bone growth.

Physical Inactivity   Immobility can be a serious threat to your bones. Consider the following: Only 36 weeks in bed following an accident or traumatic illness is equivalent to ten years of aging on your bones. And it's hard work to put those bone-years back once they're gone.

To maintain healthy bone structure, moderate exercise on a regular basis (daily is best!) is recommended. One study showed that women who participated in a moderate exercise program three to four times a week had greater bone density than those who didn't or who exercised less. Weight-bearing exercise has been found to be a real benefit in the prevention of osteoporosis. Bones need to be stressed to grow stronger (this is the "use it or lose it" theory), as do the muscles surrounding the bones.

Childlessness   A life-style factor that isn't easy to alter is pregnancy. Apparently, the hormonal changes that the body experiences during the growth and maturation of a fetus are influential on bone remodeling. Bone density increases during a woman's pregnancy—it's almost as if the body were securing the house for the new inhabitant. (One contributing factor is that most women ingest at least four eight-ounce glasses of milk daily during their pregnancies. For some, this may be the most calcium they've ever had in their lives!)

Prolonged Lactation If you nurse your child for several years, you are depleting your own body of its calcium more quickly than women in their reproductive years who wean their children quickly. So prolonged lactation can cause bone loss.

Lack of Fluoride One last life-style factor has to do with environment. If you live in an area where the local water is treated with sodium fluoride, your bones as well as your teeth may be stronger. Some studies done in towns with and without fluoride-treated water indicate that there are fewer fractures overall and particularly in older women in areas with treated water. Other studies contradict this finding; so the jury is still out on how influential this factor may be.

Age-Associated Factors

- Menopausal
- Elderly

Menopausal We've already talked about sex-related differences in osteoporosis, but the gap between the sexes is most striking between the ages of 50 and 70. Osteoporosis may set in following menopause, when a woman's ovaries slow down and eventually stop producing the protective hormone estrogen. As you may recall from Chapter 1, estrogen is greatly responsible for keeping calcium within the bone tissue. For five or ten years after menopause, women lose bone density at a rapid rate—most lose at about 1 to 3 percent a year, but some faster bone losers may drop as much as 6 percent a year. Then, at 70 or so, when the body reaches a new hormonal balance, the rate slows down to about 1 to 2 percent a year. All in all, women can lose 30 percent of their cortical bone and up to 50 percent of their trabecular bone over this time.

Elderly   Past age 75, both men and women can be at risk for osteoporosis. Remember that aging affects all bones—male and female—and elderly bones tend to be frail and porous in men as well as women at this age. Then, too, older people tend to exercise less, and many of their medications may make them drowsy or unaware of their surroundings or affect their balance, making them prone to falling.

Medical Factors

- Surgical menopause (if you've had both ovaries removed and are no longer producing estrogen)

- Taking glucocorticoid drugs

- Regular use of antacids that contain aluminum

Surgical Menopause   Women who have had both ovaries removed are at great risk, particularly following their operation.

In this surgical procedure, called an *oophorectomy,* the ovaries, those reproductive organs responsible for hormone production, are excised. If all the reproductive organs—uterus, cervix, fallopian tubes, and ovaries—are removed, the procedure is called a *TAHBSO* (*total abdominal hysterectomy and bilateral salpingo-oophorectomy*). In either case, hormonal production stops, except for the small amount of hormones still generated by the adrenal glands (see Chapter 9). This procedure creates an early menopause, which means a lack of estrogen circulating through the body. A natural menopause ensures that the body has time to adjust to new hormonal levels, since the slowing-down process of the reproductive system may take several years. But a surgical menopause occurs instantly, giving the body no time to adjust to the new hormonal levels. So the bone formation and resorption cycle is immediately affected.

Glucocorticoid Drugs and Antacids   Glucocorticoids and other drugs that weaken bone, such as anticonvulsants, present another medical risk factor. If you have a chronic disease that requires you to take these drugs, you should be consulting a physician about the lowest possible dosage. Another medical risk factor is present if you take antacids that contain aluminum on a regular basis. Aluminum inhibits proper bone remodeling and adversely affects the kidneys. These drug-related risk factors, and other special cases, will be discussed in Chapter 9.

AVOIDING UNNECESSARY RISKS

You can't change your age, sex, or race. But you certainly *can* make positive changes in other areas. If you've been a smoker all your life, preventing osteoporosis is a terrific reason to stop right now. If you've always felt an urge to crash diet before a wedding or special event so that you can fit into a special outfit, this is the time to correct this destructive nutritional behavior. If you're a chronic couch potato, you can wake up tomorrow and start walking a brisk two miles a day. You can start supplementing your calcium intake and make sure you get out in the sunshine every day, too.

The life-style changes you make can alter your osteoporosis profile, even if you fit into every one of the genetic categories. You can turn back the clock and forestall the disease for 10 or 20 years by taking steps to give your bones the best possible chance. The possibilities of avoiding or deferring osteoporosis until 80 or even later instead of having it at 70 or 60 are *real* and will make a significant difference in the quality of your life.

THREE

WHO ARE THE TYPICAL OSTEOPOROSIS PATIENTS?

There are many different candidates for this disease, at many different ages and stages of life. You can be as young as 25 or as old as 100. You may be a Caucasian postmenopausal woman or a young Hispanic man with a hormone deficiency.

If you don't know that you have a disease, it may seem illogical to seek medical advice. However, when the disease is osteoporosis, where early detection—perhaps before any of the symptoms of this disease appear—is crucial, you might want to see a doctor even if you don't think you need to.

Remember that bones grow and remodel very slowly. If you give yourself the gift of time by having your condition professionally monitored by a knowledgeable health-care provider, you may be able to save yourself years of disabling pain and thousands of dollars in long-term care.

Let's look at some typical cases.

DIAGNOSING PATIENTS
BEFORE FRACTURE

Margaret, 40 years old, in good health. Her mother has suffered five fractures (including two vertebrae, a wrist, and a rib) in the last eight years.

Margaret's new gynecologist knows when she walks into the office that this patient has several risk factors for osteoporosis: She is blonde and blue-eyed, about five feet two inches, and extremely—perhaps excessively—thin. The doctor takes a family history and learns about Margaret's mother. She decides that at this stage, even though Margaret has a few years to go before menopause, it would be very helpful for her to have a baseline bone densitometry measurement (see Chapter 4 for a description of this noninvasive test). This way, both patient and physician will know whether family history is playing a big part or a small part in Margaret's osteoporosis profile. And knowing that, the two of them can make an informed decision about treatment. The physician mentions that many women begin taking hormones (estrogen and progesterone) even before their menses have stopped. The course of medication supplements and, then, after menopause, replaces the body's natural production of the hormones essential to good bone health. (See Chapter 7 for a discussion of hormone replacement therapy [HRT].)

The doctor asks Margaret for a detailed description of her nutrition and exercise regimens and asks whether she takes supplemental calcium. When she discovers that Margaret is very concerned about her weight, she asks her about yo-yo dieting, and Margaret tells her that she skips meals and occasionally "starves" herself before a special occasion.

Then the physician asks Margaret if she would consider taking replacement hormones if testing found that she was losing bone mass and density at this point. Margaret says she would consider it.

The doctor's recommendations are the following:

1. A bone densitometry test of both hip and spine. By actually having a reading of her bone mass and density, the doctor would be able to tell if Margaret is losing bone faster than most women her age.

2. A sensible and regular diet, stressing complex carbohydrates (whole grains, vegetables, and fruits, particularly those foods high in calcium); less animal protein; more vegetable protein like peas, beans, and other legumes; and a small amount of fats (including dairy products high in calcium).

3. A regular exercise program. Not a killer regimen but at least 20 minutes of walking, jogging, biking, or aerobics daily. She tells her that she should also consider light weight training and stair climbing.

4. Supplemental calcium—1,000 mg of calcium citrate or carbonate daily, taken with or just after meals for proper absorption.

5. She tells her they'll talk about hormone replacement therapy when she gets the results of the test.

Jennifer, 48 years old, in good health, a two-pack-a-day smoker, doesn't exercise. Mother is no longer living but had osteoporosis and spent the last few years of her life in a wheelchair.

Jennifer has missed several periods in the last year and has experienced her first few hot flashes. She decides it's time to discuss her osteoporosis profile with her physician.

The doctor does a history and learns that Jennifer does eat a fairly balanced diet but one that is low in calcium. She has tried to stop smoking many times over the years but has never stuck with her resolve. She's always hated exercise and even drives to the mailbox at the end of her long driveway instead of walking. Her chronic fatigue lately seems to make it harder to get motivated—either to stop smoking or to start exercising.

She has heard that taking supplemental hormones at this time of life often supplies extra energy and wants to know if that's true and if it would work for her. She's also concerned about the fact that her mother had osteoporosis.

The doctor's recommendations are the following:

1. Get into a good nonsmoking program and kick the smoking habit forever. This may mean a combination of physical methods (the nicotine patch or gum, for example) and motivational help. It may mean finding a stress-reduction activity such as meditation, tai chi, or self-hypnosis.

2. Increase calcium-rich foods and take supplemental calcium in order to obtain 1,000 mg daily.

3. Begin walking. It's the easiest activity for inveterate couch potatoes. The best way to stop making excuses and really start exercising is to set aside one time segment a day specifically reserved for exercise. Setting the alarm 20 minutes earlier is one good tactic to try, since it's been found that most people find it easier to

exercise early in the day. If Jennifer has an active social life and enjoys doing things with friends, she might want to consider a team sport like volleyball, a partner sport like tennis or racquetball, or any kind of dancing. She might also join a health club or walkers' club so she can exercise with other people.

The doctor assures Jennifer that her chronic fatigue will start to fade as the exercise program takes hold. Even moderate daily exercise triggers the *beta endorphins* in the brain, those natural opiates that make us feel good. He also assures her that she can change her genetic risk factor. Though family history certainly plays a part, Jennifer is starting early enough in her preventive care to reduce her chances of developing the osteoporosis her mother had.

4. Have a bone densitometry test. This will show both doctor and patient what Jennifer's current bone mass and density are and how they compare with other women's in her age-group. If her test results are low, he may recommend that she start taking estrogen and progesterone. He confirms the fact that supplemental estrogen can make women feel less fatigued, but his major interest in this type of medication is the protection it offers for Jennifer's bones and heart as she moves toward menopause.

If her densitometry readings are normal, however, the doctor will see her in a year at her next regular gynecological examination. At that point, they will repeat the bone densitometry test and see whether HRT might be in order at that point.

Sally, 53, in good health, past menopause, former smoker and crash dieter.

The gynecologist notes that Sally refused hormone replacement therapy two years ago because she "just didn't feel right about it." He orders a biochemical analysis of blood and urine. Then the doctor sends Sally to the nuclear medicine department at his hospital to have a bone densitometry test done on both her hip and her spine and discovers that she has normal bone mass for her age. She is taking daily calcium, now eats a good diet, and takes a martial arts class twice a week. She does a lot of walking, too.

The doctor's recommendations are the following:

1. He advises her to keep up her exercise program and to start some light weight training at a local gym as an alternative activity.

2. He goes over her diet with her to be certain she's getting enough dietary calcium, cautions her not to go on any crash diets, and reminds her it's not a bad idea to carry five extra pounds after the menopause, both as protective padding against falls and for enhanced estrone production.

3. He boosts her supplemental calcium requirement to 1,500 mg of calcium daily.

4. He once again recommends that she consider hormone replacement therapy, showing her ample documentation that taking supplemental estrogen at this time in her life when she is losing bone rapidly can effectively slow or stop the bone loss. This time she decides to start wearing a transdermal estrogen patch and taking a progesterone supplement by mouth.

Pia, 25 years old, recently had both ovaries surgically removed because of severe (stage IV) endometriosis, has fibrocystic breasts but otherwise is in good health, slightly overweight, only exercises during the summer when she can swim in her town pool.

The doctor discussed supplemental estrogen with Pia before her operation, and when she comes in for her follow-up six weeks after surgery, he strongly recommends it. Since she has no ovaries, she is no longer producing estrogen, and her lack of hormonal protection will immediately put her at risk for heart disease and osteoporosis. Pia mentions her fibrocystic breasts (breasts with benign lumps) and wonders if taking estrogen may increase her risk of breast cancer. Fibrocystic breasts do make it harder for a physician to pick up a malignant lump and therefore to detect cancer at an early stage.

The doctor tells her that recent studies show that low-dose estrogen use does not increase the risk of breast cancer in women with benign breast disease. Since Pia is just 25 years old, 10 years before her bone growth will reach its peak, she will begin to lose bone density rapidly because she is undergoing an early menopause. Naturally, the physician will monitor her breasts carefully to make sure there is no change due to her taking estrogen. The hormone replacement will also circumvent other menopausal symptoms she would naturally experience, such as hot flashes and vaginal atrophy.

The doctor's recommendations are the following:

1. A mammogram. The doctor points out that if he should see anything in the breast examination that would make him cautious about prescribing estrogen replacement, Pia has the option of taking injectable calcitonin as a preventive measure against osteoporosis. Calcitonin will not take care of other menopausal

symptoms, but it will protect her bones. (See Chapter 7, "Medical Treatments.")

2. Oral hormone replacement therapy (as long as the results of the mammogram prove normal).

3. A balanced diet, high in calcium.

4. A regular, nonstressful exercise program, including activities that will increase her aerobic capacity, her flexibility, and her strength. He suggests that although swimming is fine, it is not weight bearing and therefore she should combine it with a walking or bicycling program.

5. Supplemental calcium, 1,000 mg daily (high for her age-group but the appropriate dosage for a menopausal woman on replacement hormones).

6. A biochemical analysis and bone densitometry test within a year.

DIAGNOSIS AFTER A FRACTURE

If you are at high risk for osteoporosis and you have sustained a fracture, you have less leeway on the timing of your care because your disease is more advanced. Osteoporosis typically strikes postmenopausal women in their fifties (or earlier, if their ovaries were surgically removed). This disease strikes midlife women as their trabecular bone becomes fragile and porous. After age 75, both men and women can be affected by the disease as the aging process causes both trabecular and cortical bone to thin out.

Postmenopausal Osteoporosis—
Fracture of the Trabecular Bone

Women from 51 to 65 may lose bone rapidly as their estrogen production drops off and be extremely susceptible to fracturing the inner, spongy portion of bone that becomes more porous after menopause. When there is less estrogen in the body, old bone tissue is eaten away faster than new bone is laid down (the process known as *resorption*). Typically, the forearm (radius) will break (Colles' fracture), or a vertebra will collapse. What's happened is that the interior structure of the bone has become so fragile that it can no longer support the weight put on it by the rest of the skeleton, and it collapses under pressure. A woman who puts out her arm to catch herself as she falls can fracture her wrist; a woman who simply sneezes can get a vertebral compression fracture.

The loss sustained in this type of bone accelerates as we get older, particularly in women for the five or ten years after menopause. (Women may lose up to 50 percent of this type of bone throughout their lifetime. Men, who have a much higher proportion of bone mass to begin with, lose only insignificant amounts of it up to age 75 or so, because the levels of their protective hormone, testosterone, remain pretty stable throughout midlife.)

Elderly Osteoporosis—Fracture of
Both Trabecular and Cortical Bone

Elderly people over age 75 may get osteoporosis due to the generally slow aging process of both trabecular and cortical bone. Some women, who were protected by naturally high levels of estrogen in their bodies postmen-

Compression fractures of the vertebrae in elderly people lead to loss of height and "dowager's hump." Eventually, downward pressure on the organs will cause abdominal distension.

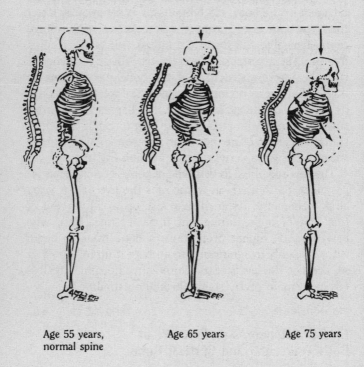

Age 55 years,
normal spine

Age 65 years

Age 75 years

opausally, may not have suffered any early fractures. But now as they age, they may become susceptible to breaks of the upper arm, shin bone, pelvis, and particularly the hip. (Other women who suffered fractures during their fifties may experience another sequence of breaks in later life.)

As men live longer, they, too, may develop osteoporosis. Their testosterone levels do decrease—although slowly— in old age, and the remodeling process of replacing old bone with new bone slows or halts during the aging process. The incidence of increased mortality in connection with hip fractures in older people is staggering—12 to 20 percent of those who break a hip die within one year.

Cortical bone is the type found in the shafts of the long bones of the body. The loss we sustain in this type of bone peaks at about age 65. (Women usually lose about 35 percent of their cortical bone throughout their lifetimes.)

Let's look at some patients and their diagnoses.

Mary, 67, has asthma and therefore has had problems sticking to an exercise program. She fell on the uneven pavement outside her house and broke her wrist.

The first time Mary ever mentioned any lower back pain was after she broke her wrist. She was treated in an emergency room, and a cast was put on her lower arm. When she went to her family doctor to have the cast removed, she was clearly in a lot of discomfort and had trouble getting up on the examining table.

The doctor does the following:

1. Her physician puts a new soft cast on her wrist, which has been healing very slowly, and tells her to wear it in a sling whenever she's doing any activity that might jar it.

2. He orders a bone densitometry test on her hip and spine and is able to see from the results that her bone mass and density are quite low, in the lowest third of her age-group.

3. He puts Mary on a regular walking program and recommends a diet high in calcium.

4. He also recommends calcium supplementation: 1,500 mg daily. Since Mary doesn't get outside in the sunshine as much as she should, he also prescribes vitamin D, 800 mg daily.

5. He suggests that Mary start hormone replacement therapy to slow down the process of further bone loss, and Mary, seeing the results of her densitometry test, agrees.

6. He recommends a physical therapist who works with patients who have osteoporosis to teach her lower back exercises.

7. He asks her to make an appointment to see him after six months to evaluate her treatment.

Aaron, 92, broken hip, uses a walker, very frail and fragile but motivated to take care of himself. In the past ten years, he has suffered several vertebral fractures as well. (He lives with his daughter, son-in-law, and two grandchildren.)

The doctor notes that Aaron has not improved or declined physically since his last visit but that he seems slightly depressed and claims to be forgetful about taking his calcium and vitamin D. On the nights that his family is out at Cub Scout meetings or classes, he falls asleep and rarely eats. He is also embarrassed about the fact that he wet his bed one night when he couldn't get to the bathroom in time.

The doctor recommends the following:

1. His daughter prepare meals for him and set an alarm clock to go off at mealtime on the nights they're not home.

2. He suggests a bedpan for under Aaron's bed to relieve his stress about getting to the bathroom when he feels he can't make it in time.

3. He suggests that his vitamin/mineral supplement be placed on his breakfast tray so he can't forget to take it.

4. He prescribes short-term physical therapy to give Aaron exercises he can do seated in a chair or in bed.

5. He suggests that Aaron be taken regularly to a senior center or a class of his choice so that he can interact socially with people other than his family members.

ANYONE CAN BE A CANDIDATE FOR OSTEOPOROSIS

From the wide range of patients discussed in this chapter, it should be clear that osteoporosis is a disease that strikes young and old, male and female. And because it remains silent in the body for such a long time before any damage is noticed, it is often difficult to catch at an early stage.

But the sooner it's caught and the sooner treatment begins, the better your chances of controlling it.

FOUR

BIOCHEMICAL AND DENSITOMETRY TESTING

Osteoporosis is not always an easy disease to diagnose, so it is of the utmost importance that you choose a physician who will recognize the symptoms, is aware of the appropriate tests, and will recommend medication, exercise, diet, and other modalities of care. This chapter will explain how to find the right physician and what tests he or she might perform to determine whether you have osteoporosis. Together, you and your physician will become partners in good preventive care and treatment.

SYMPTOMS THAT INDICATE YOU MAY ALREADY HAVE OSTEOPOROSIS

You may initially go to your family physician complaining of one or several of the following symptoms:

- Bone pain
- Lower back pain

- A fracture of the wrist, hip, or spine that won't heal

- Cramps in legs and feet, particularly at night

- Dowager's hump (*kyphosis*), a definite rounding of the upper spine (this indicates that several vertebrae have fractured and moved out of alignment)

- Loss of height (meaning that one or several vertebrae have collapsed)

- Extreme fatigue

- Periodontal disease

- Very brittle fingernails

- Rheumatic pains in the limbs, spine, and pelvis, combined with anemia

These are symptoms that *might* indicate you have osteoporosis. But there is no sure sign that will allow you to make this diagnosis yourself. Other diseases have similar —sometimes identical—symptoms.

The process of losing bone density is so gradual and insidious that the only way to tell how far your condition has already progressed is to consult a specialist and go through diagnostic testing. But what kind of physician should you select?

FINDING THE RIGHT PHYSICIAN

Since osteoporosis is a disease that generally affects mid-life women and older women and men, you will need to find a doctor who treats patients in these age-groups. And although osteoporosis involves bone, it is also a hormonally regulated disease. This means that your first source of counsel should be your regular gynecologist. This physician will be able to treat you or will refer you elsewhere. He or she might send you to an osteoporosis clinic if you happen to be fortunate enough to live near one (see Chapter 11); a menopause clinic, where all aspects of postmenopausal health are considered; an endocrinologist who understands the hormonal changes that occur during midlife and later; a rheumatologist who is concerned with the health of the musculoskeletal system; or if you are 65 or older, an internist who treats older individuals, or a geriatrician.

Any of the physicians you might consult for this condition should be state licensed and board-certified in their specialty. You can check on their credentials (medical school graduation, internship, residency, and fellowship) in a state medical specialty directory, available in the reference section of your library. You can also call your state medical board.

Hospital affiliation is also important to consider. Since the only absolute indication of the condition of your bone tissue is a reading from a bone densitometry test, you will need the physician you select to be affiliated with a hospital, clinic, or medical center where this equipment is available. (Dedicated osteoporosis and menopause clinics and many rheumatology and endocrinology practices have such a machine on premises, in their offices.)

WHY WOULD TESTING BE NECESSARY?

There are two reasons your doctor might wish to do both biochemical (blood and urine) and radiological tests.

1. You are suffering from any of the symptoms listed above and your doctor wishes to rule out other diseases. If you have already broken a wrist or hip, these tests would not be done as a diagnostic procedure for osteoporosis since it's clear that you do, in fact, have brittle bones. But if you are in a very low risk category and have a pattern of fractures—for example, if you are a young man or an Afro-American or Hispanic woman —your doctor may do a radiological study as well as a bone density analysis to see whether your problem is due to, say, metastatic cancer or some bone problem other than osteoporosis.

2. Around the time of your menopause, or several years prior, when you first begin to experience irregular menses or hot flashes, your gynecologist might ask whether you have considered taking replacement hormones in order to protect your bones and your heart as you age. In order to find out whether you are in a high-risk category for osteoporosis, and to determine the suitability of hormone treatment, the doctor might recommend a blood test to determine your current hormonal level and a bone densitometry test.

A baseline test for bone density, just like a baseline mammogram, is a good barometer of what you can expect in the future. If the tests determine that you are in the normal range, you may not have to see a physician for another year or two. If subsequent tests determine that you are losing bone mass and density at a rapid rate, your physician can immediately get you on a course of treatment. After you've been treated for a year, you can have an easy follow-up test to be sure that the program you're on is right for you.

BIOCHEMICAL TESTING

Before sending you for a bone density test, the doctor will want to ensure that there are no disease processes going on in your body that might affect your bone tissue. He or she will then draw blood and ask for a urine sample in order to do specific biochemical tests.

Your physician will not do all these tests. The ones your physician recommends for you will depend on your own health status and any other medical problems he or she suspects may be affecting your bone profile.

Blood Tests

Your doctor will order *blood tests* to measure red and white blood cell counts, as well as protein, calcium, phosphorus, parathyroid and thyroid hormone levels, and vitamin D levels (both active and inactive). He or she may also wish to do liver and kidney function tests. Because blood, hormones, protein, and bone tissue all interact, it's important to have a general profile of these levels.

This profile will also help to rule out other diseases. It is important for your physician to know whether you are suffering from thyroid or parathyroid disease, any abnormality of the adrenal glands, cancer of the bone marrow (myeloma), or softening of the bones (adult rickets). Any abnormal levels in the blood tests might indicate that more specialized testing should be done for these diseases.

Testing for Hormone Levels

As we've said, the loss of estrogen after menopause puts midlife women at risk for osteoporosis. For this reason, it's essential for your doctor to know the level of endogenous estrogen (the amount of estrogen naturally circulating in the body) if you are past menopause. Your doctor will therefore test your *estradiol* level (estradiol is the kind of estrogen your body manufactures naturally) and also possibly your pituitary hormone levels, *follicle-stimulate hormone* (*FSH*) and *luteinizing hormone* (*LH*). If your estrogen level is low, this may indicate that hormone replacement therapy is advisable. It will also encourage your physician to go further with diagnostic testing by ordering a densitometry reading.

Urine Tests

The specialized urine test for osteoporosis measures the ratio between calcium and creatinine in your urine. Creatinine, one of the nonprotein constituents of blood, remains stable throughout your life. When your doctor examines the results of a *24-hour urinary calcium and creatinine excretion* test, he or she can tell what losses have occurred in the amount of calcium collected. If your urinary calcium is high, the doctor knows that you are losing calcium instead of absorbing it properly so that it can assist in the bone remodeling process. (In order to take this test, you must carry a jug around with you for a day and void into it.)

The more specific tests for bone turnover and resorption are also important in your initial diagnosis and in the follow-up of your treatment. To find out how quickly bone is being formed, the doctor may order a *serum total* or *bone-specific alkaline phosphatase* test, a *serum osteocalcin* test, and a serum level of a certain kind of *collagen propeptide.*

To find out how quickly bone is being resorbed, a doctor may order a *hydroxyproline* test. New and very sensitive tests for this measurement are *pyridinoline* and *deoxypyridinoline,* which are specific for certain types of collagen. These might be performed on an elderly patient who has just suffered a sudden rash of fractures.

Repeating these pyridinoline tests a year or two after therapy has begun will show how effective medication, diet (including calcium supplementation), and exercise have been.

Predictions for Your Future

Certain studies indicate that these baseline biochemical markers, along with a densitometry reading of bone mass, can not only indicate what's happening presently in the body but may be able to estimate the rate of bone loss for the next decade. Right now, it does not seem certain that a single measurement of bone turnover will predict what it will be next week, next month, or next year. But as researchers develop better markers for bone formation and resorption, it may be possible to predict the time in a patient's life when fractures might start to occur. Having this knowledge, a doctor would make sure that those most at risk begin treatment early on.

X-RAY MEASUREMENT

If you've had a traditional X ray because your doctor wants to rule out causes of back pain such as osteoarthritis or metastatic cancer, and your doctor discovers that you have vertebral fractures, you will probably be put on hormone replacement therapy or calcitonin injections at once. However, it is not possible to tell if you have osteoporosis by taking an ordinary X ray if you don't have fractures. Bone loss doesn't show up with this type of measurement until it reaches nearly 30 percent. If your doctor does see this kind of significant loss on an X ray, your disease is already quite advanced, and there is no question that you should be in treatment.

BONE DENSITOMETRY

Densitometry is used for diagnosis and for monitoring your condition. The diagnosis of your condition comes from the comparison of your bone density to accepted norms; the monitoring capability comes from repeating this test over time, either to see how fast you are losing bone or to see how well you are responding to therapy.

Bone mineral density shows up as a radiographic picture on a computer screen. The scan shows the bone mineral content and bone mineral density you have and gives readings on a computer printout for each area examined —the spine, the hip, or the forearm. From these measurements, the machine does an estimate of where your *fracture threshold* is greatest, and the computer screen shows a crosshatch on your danger areas: Beneath the cross, you are at risk; above the cross, you are still in the normal, safe range. If your physician has you repeat this test in a year or two, a comparison can be made between the tests to figure out the rate at which bone is being lost.

Since bone mineral density (BMD) values decline naturally as we get older, the doctor wants to see if your values are greater than or equal to the norm for your age. With repeated measurements, he or she can see, for example, if after menopause you are losing in the 1 to 3 percent range—pretty standard—or if you are in the high-risk 5 to 6 percent range and should start a course of treatment. The doctor can also see whether you are maintaining or even gaining bone density after being on your treatment program for a year.

The Four Types of Densitometry Machines

Densitometry machines are most often found in the nuclear medicine departments of major medical centers or university hospitals in moderately large cities. Even physicians in small towns and rural areas may have access to single-photon absorptiometry machines (see description below). Insurance will only cover these tests if they are part of a diagnostic procedure for a suspected disease condition—not as preventive care for osteoporosis. The tests will run from $75 to $250, depending on which part of the country you live in, how many areas of the body are being examined, and which machine your physician is using.

There are currently four methods of assessing the bone mineral density of your skeleton and, from this, your risk of fracture. All these noninvasive procedures are safe and painless.

The four types of measurement are:

- Single-photon absorptiometry (SPA)

- Dual-energy photon absorptiometry (DPA)

- Dual-energy X-ray absorptiometry (DEXA or DXA)

- Quantitative computed tomography (QCT)

Single-photon absorptiometry (*SPA*) uses a radioactive isotope to give a picture of the bone. For a reading on an SPA machine, you sit beside a table and place your wrist or forearm under the scanner. A picture of your bone will appear on the computer screen in front of the technician across the room. When the machine completes the scan, it analyzes bone mass and density and compares it to statistically normal bone.

In this test, photons are passed through the wrist, forearm, or elbow from one radioactive source to determine bone mass and density at that site. This is the least expensive of the procedures; however, it only tells the doctor a little bit about your osteoporosis profile, since it only examines one part of your body and only shows the density in the cortical bone. Some newer equipment exists that can look at the trabecular bone in the end or distal part of the forearm.

A more precise but more expensive test is *dual-energy photon absorptiometry* (*DPA*), which uses a dual-energy isotope and passes beams from two radioactive sources through your body. It can look at thicker parts of your body, such as the spine, the hip, and even the total body mass, and make an assessment about mass and density of both cortical and trabecular bone. It takes approximately twice as long to get a reading on this kind of equipment as it does on the DEXA (see below), which makes the procedure less cost-effective. Also, you can only look at the spine straight on with this machine. Lateral spine scanning—a side view—cannot be taken on this type of equipment.

Dual-energy X ray absorptiometry (*DEXA* or *DXA*) is the state-of-the-art method of measuring bone density. Currently, the equipment is only available in major urban areas, but the machines are being adopted at an increasing rate around the country. As is clear from its name, the machine uses an X-ray source rather than an isotope source. It is more accurate, takes less time, and gives the patient a much lower dosage of radiation. A typical first scan would be a picture of your lower lumbar region (the base of the spine) and your wrist. Typically, the procedure would take from two to four minutes, depending on your size and the thickness of your tissue.

For a reading of your spine or hip on a DPA, or DEXA, you lie on your back on the table with your legs draped over a raised box. The readings generally taken are *anterior/posterior* (AP). Occasionally, the doctor may also request a lateral view as you lie on your side. This can be done on a DEXA.

The *quantitative computed tomography* (*QCT*) *scanner* —basically a CT scanner with specialized software—is the most expensive method, takes the longest time, and exposes you to higher doses of radiation. The machine is usually used to measure the lumbar spine. These machines do not give measurements as precise as the DEXA measurements, although they do provide a cross-sectional look at the vertebrae, which allows for measurement of the trabecular bone. Since the turnover rate in this type of bone is nearly eight times that of cortical bone, this technique was of interest to doctors before the DEXA was available because it offered early detection of osteoporotic changes in the body.

During a QCT scan, you are placed inside a large hollow

tube on the table and must lie very still—for up to 15 minutes—as your body is analyzed by the scanner inside.

How Does the Doctor Use Densitometry Readings?

By comparing your values with a previously determined norm, the doctor can determine how fast you are losing bone density, and the two of you can decide together whether you should be in therapy or whether you should wait a year and have another measurement done.

The two of you will use your biochemical test results and bone density measurements to get a well-rounded picture of those elements that may predict later problems. By making these determinations early on, you will have some meaningful parameters to help you decide on your alternatives for the future.

Techniques for the Measurement of Bone Mass

Technique	Site	Precision (%)	Accuracy (%)	Examination Time (minutes)	Dose of Radiation* (mrem)	Approximate Cost ($)
Single-photon absorptiometry (SPA)	Wrist, heel	1–3	5	15	10–20	75–150
Dual-energy photon absorptiometry (DPA)	Spine, hip, total body	2–4	4–10	20–40	5	150–200
Dual-energy X-ray absorptiometry (DXA)	Spine, hip, total body	0.5–2	3–5	3–7	1–3	150–200
Quantitative computed tomography (QCT)	Spine	2–5	5–20	10–15	100–300	150–250

*One chest X ray gives a radiation dose of 20 to 50 mrem (milli-roentgen-equivalent-man); a full dental X ray, 300 mrem; and an abdominal CT, 1 to 6 rem.

Credit: National Osteoporosis Foundation

FIVE

HELP YOURSELF: THE PREVENTIVE DIET AND EXERCISE PROGRAM

The best treatment for osteoporosis can't be purchased in a drugstore. It comes from establishing and maintaining a regular program of good personal health throughout your life. In this chapter, we'll describe the benefits of a nutritious diet, a daily exercise program, and vitamin and mineral supplementation.

Your Eight-Step Preventive Plan for Better Bones

1. Eat a balanced high-calcium, high-fiber, low-fat, low–animal protein diet.

2. Never go on crash diets.

3. Keep your weight about five pounds higher than it was before menopause once you have stopped having periods, especially if you are thin and have a small frame.

4. Engage in a *daily* program of weight-bearing exercise that stresses your bones and muscles without knocking you out.

5. Stop smoking—and stay smoke-free the rest of your life.

6. Cut down or cut out alcohol.

7. Cut down or cut out caffeine (found in coffee, tea, cocoa, and many soft drinks).

8. Cut down or cut out processed foods and high-phosphate sodas.

A HEALTHY LIFE-STYLE IS THE BEST MEDICINE

It's only recently that Americans have realized the benefits of *preventive medicine*—that is, warding off or forestalling illness by leading a healthy life-style. For the past ten years or so, you've heard a great deal about the importance of tending and nourishing your body with a proper diet and exercise. This is particularly true in the prevention of osteoporosis, a disease that can be thwarted by a strong, well-nourished body in good biochemical and mechanical balance.

If you take care of your body, your body will serve you better as you age. When you're in good physical shape, you are less susceptible to debilitating chronic diseases. If you maintain a good diet and exercise plan, you may forestall osteoporosis for ten years or more and prevent falls that may lead to fractures. Calcium-rich foods supply bone tissue with needed nutrients; weight-bearing exercise strengthens bone and muscle and makes joints and tendons more flexible.

What you weigh can also play a part in your total bone profile. Unfortunately, we have all been brainwashed into believing that Madison Avenue's vision of emaciated beauty is one that we should emulate. The most misguided maxim of our youth- and money-oriented culture is, You can never be too rich or too thin.

The truth is, as you get past menopause (or if you are a man over age 75), you *can* be too thin. It is far better to carry an extra five pounds, rich in those fat cells that convert androstenedione into estrones, than it is to try to squeeze into your old size-8 jeans. This is not to say that being fat is desirable, because obesity causes a host of other problems. But a little additional padding in your later years is a good idea as protection against breaks.

It's very important that you have sufficient vitamin D, which you can get from a walk in the sunshine (wear sunscreen to prevent overexposure to ultraviolet rays). You can also take vitamin D in tablet form, as a dietary supplement.

NUTRITIONAL BALANCE

As you grow older, your body handles the nutrients you ingest in different ways. You don't burn calories as effectively because your body converts more food to fat and less to muscle and bone tissue. As your risk increases for high blood pressure and heart disease, it's more important to cut down on salt and caffeine. Your liver becomes less capable of excreting bile and has difficulty processing fatty foods, as well as alcohol, which, in excess, can damage it. For these reasons, it's important to modify what you eat and drink as you age.

Protein

You don't need as much protein as you get older. It's particularly important to cut down on red meat or avoid it altogether because it is high in fat and it increases the rate of urinary calcium excretion. Many foods in the American diet are processed with phosphates, and excess phosphorus is detrimental to bone (see pages 69–70).

Complex Carbohydrates

Increase your complex carbohydrates. Make sure your diet includes plenty of high-fiber cereal, pasta (without creamy sauces), rice, and potatoes. Complex carbohydrates are also found in fruits and vegetables; eat plenty of both categories, preferably fresh, not frozen or canned.

Fats

A substantial amount of scientific evidence has shown that excess fat in the diet causes a variety of problems from heart disease and stroke to obesity. A well-rounded diet should contain less than 30 percent of its calories from fat. Stick to monosaturated or polyunsaturated fats and cut down or cut out saturated fats.

Simple Starches and Sugars

Refined and processed starches, such as white flour and white rice, have been robbed of the fiber that your body needs. Refined white sugar—sucrose—appears in an amazing number of products that don't even taste sweet. Unlike fructose, the sugar in whole fruits, it has no redeeming value other than tasting good. Read the labels on everything you buy, from salad dressing to crackers! Simple starches and sugars provide only empty calories. Cut them out or keep them to a minimum.

NO MORE CIGARETTES

Smokers have been known to go through menopause as much as five years earlier than nonsmokers. They are at higher risk for many forms of cancer and for cardiovascular disease. They also tend to complain of many more discomforts. If you smoke, this means five extra years of estrogen depletion and five more years of losing bone mass. Smokers tend to be thinner, and thinner women have fewer, smaller fat cells manufacturing estrones (the "watered-down" estrogen) after menopause. Smoking also doubles the amount of calcium excreted back into the bloodstream.

In the process of smoking, the bloodstream is robbed of an adequate oxygen supply. The capillaries, therefore, are unable to supply sufficient nourishment to the bone tissue. Smoking interferes with healing, no matter what the ailment or injury. Smokers have been shown to have up to 25 percent more degeneration of the intervertebral disks in the spinal column than nonsmokers. Cigarettes also negate or offset the effectiveness of hormone replacement therapy.

Because of all the additional hazards (and expense!) cigarettes present, the wisest course is to *stop smoking now*.

MINERALS AND VITAMINS CRUCIAL TO BONES: DIETARY SOURCES

Minerals

Calcium (The National Osteoporosis Foundation recommends 1,000 mg of calcium daily for all adults and women on HRT and recommends 1,500 mg daily for postmenopausal women not taking HRT and for men over 75.) Good dietary sources of calcium are:

Dairy: low-fat milk, cheese, and yogurt

Fish with bones: sardines, mackerel, and salmon

Green leafy vegetables: bok choy; kale; and collard, mustard, and turnip greens. Although spinach is also high in calcium, its high phytic acid content makes it difficult for the body to absorb.

Other green vegetables: seaweed (kelp) like Japanese nori, broccoli, brussels sprouts, and cabbage

Nuts and legumes: all beans and peas such as kidney, lima, navy, and soybeans, sunflower seeds, tofu and tempeh, pecans, walnuts, almonds, and peanuts

Yellow vegetables: turnips and squashes

Cereals: farina

The Calcium Content of Foods

Food	mg Calcium
Whole milk, 8 oz	291
1% fortified milk, 8 oz	349
Nonfat dry milk, ¼ cup	377
Yogurt, plain low-fat, 1 cup	414
Yogurt, plain, nonfat, 1 cup	452
Cheese, cheddar, 1 oz	204
Cheese, cottage, 4 oz	68
Cheese, feta, 1 oz	140
Cheese, mozzarella, part-skim, 1 oz	183
Cheese, Muenster, 1 oz	203
Collard greens, 1 cup	357
Kale, 1 cup	179
Broccoli, 1 cup	178
Swiss chard, 1 cup	102
Mustard greens, 1 cup	150
Salmon with bones, 3 oz	203
Sardines with bones, 3¼ oz	351
Oysters, 1 cup	111
Calcium-enriched orange juice, 6 oz	225

Magnesium   (The recommended daily allowance [RDA] is 400 mg, but most dietitians recommend that the amount equal about half the calcium you ingest. Therefore, if you're taking more calcium, you might wish to boost your magnesium as well.) This mineral maintains the acid/alkaline balance of the body. It's found in millet, potato, corn, wheat, brown rice, barley, and lentils. Cooking and processing washes away magnesium. (See Chapter 10 for another theory on the dietary importance of this mineral.)

Phosphorus   (The RDA is 1,000 mg.) Phosphorus is present in almost every food, and most of us eat too much of it. The more phosphorus in our diet, the more calcium we need to counteract its effects. An allied problem is that our kidneys are less able to excrete excess phosphorus as we age. As kidney function declines, parathyroid activity goes up, and higher PTH levels draw calcium out of the bones and into the bloodstream. Since processed foods are exceptionally high in phosphorus, we should try to avoid them as a general rule.

Sodium   (The RDA is 2 g [grams] daily. Most Americans consume two to three times that amount!) The kidney is responsible for conserving both sodium and calcium, and an excess of sodium will increase the loss of calcium in the urine. It's a good idea, therefore, to keep sodium intake fairly low.

Potassium   (There is no RDA.) This mineral is essential for intracellular fluid exchange and is also dependent on factors that regulate sodium balance. Without this balance between minerals, urinary calcium loss may increase. Potassium is found in lean meats, vegetables, and fruits.

Boron   (There is no RDA, but dietitians recommend 3 mg daily.) This trace mineral, found in the soil, is important in the process of calcium absorption and prevents too much urinary calcium loss. It's found in legumes, green leafy vegetables, noncitrus fruits, and nuts.

Vitamins

B-complex This is the "antistress" vitamin, which also aids to prevent fluid retention. It appears to offer all-around protection for the body, including the bones.

Vitamin B$_6$ (pyridoxine) (The RDA is 2 mg, but many dietitians recommend 5 to 10 mg daily.) This vitamin maintains the sodium-potassium balance of the body and helps sustain normal maintenance of gonadal hormones (estrogen, progesterone, and testosterone). It's found in brewer's yeast, wheat bran, organ meats, walnuts, peanuts, brown rice, and blackstrap molasses.

Vitamin D (The RDA is 400 IU [international units].) This vitamin is actually a hormone, with a molecular structure similar to that of estrogen and cortisone. It is essential to calcium absorption in the intestine, and we get it from fortified milk, oily fish (cod and herring), and sunshine. Hormones are chemical messengers, transferring information around the body through the bloodstream, and vitamin D is no exception. It initiates gene activity in many different tissues like skin cells, the pancreas, the parathyroid gland, the breasts, and ovaries, as well as the intestines and bones—its main targets. It's also involved in the body's ability to secrete insulin, which is essential for maintaining the proper blood sugar level in the body. It's important not to overload on vitamin D: high levels can be toxic.

Vitamin K This vitamin has been found to inhibit urinary calcium loss in postmenopausal women. A study conducted in The Netherlands of 1,500 women from ages 45 to 80 showed that small amounts of this vitamin—just

80 μg (micrograms) daily—could cut urinary calcium loss in half. Vitamin K is found in turnip greens, broccoli, lettuce, beef liver, brussels sprouts, and cabbage.

MINERAL AND VITAMIN SUPPLEMENTATION

As we've said, your absorption of vitamins and minerals decreases as you age. So even if you're eating a well-rounded, high-calcium diet, you may not be able to get all the benefits of what you've ingested. For this reason, supplemental minerals and vitamins are recommended, particularly for those at high risk for osteoporosis or those who've already been diagnosed with the condition.

After menopause, calcium supplements are good preventive medicine, and for elderly men and women, both calcium and vitamin D should be supplemented. Check with your doctor before adding any other food supplements to your diet. (See Chapter 7, "Medical Treatments," for a discussion of vitamins and minerals as *treatments* for osteoporosis when medication is contraindicated.)

FINDING A QUALIFIED DIETITIAN

If you are at high risk for osteoporosis or heart disease, or if you are committed to revamping your diet and don't know where to start, you should consult a professional dietitian who understands the various needs of menopausal women. A dietitian is a qualified professional in this area; someone who is listed as a "Nutritionist" may not have the same credentials or qualifications. A university hospital or medical school is your best source of referral. You can also contact the American Dietetic Association or the Center for Science in the Public Interest. (See Chapter 11, "Where to Go for Help.")

The dietitian will take a case history and do a variety of tests to determine your own dietary needs. The first step will probably be to wean you away from processed foods, refined sugar, fats, and salts. And the second step will be to give you nutritional support and correct the imbalances that exist in your system.

A DAILY EXERCISE PROGRAM

Most medical experts agree that engaging in weight-bearing exercise is essential for maintenance of good bone health throughout your life. Bones—and the muscles attached to them—need to carry weight around in order to thrive. Stressing the bones in childhood and adolescence is a big factor in how dense your bones will be at maturity, and lack of stress after menopause will cause you to lose bone mass and density faster as you age.

After only a five-month program of arm exercises practiced three times a week, a group of postmenopausal women were found to have increased their bone density, whereas the control group, who did no exercise, had lost density. Exercise also improves your balance and coordination, which will in turn protect you from falling and possibly breaking a bone.

Exercise is vital at every age because it makes you feel good about yourself, it tones and shapes your muscles, and it can provide a new social network as you meet other people who are also interested in keeping fit. Any regular exercise program gives you the added benefit of a more liberal diet, because exercise burns calories. This means you can ingest more calories as well—calcium-rich calories, of course!

WEIGHT-BEARING EXERCISE TO GUARD AGAINST OSTEOPOROSIS

Weight-bearing exercise has been shown to promote better bone deposition, make you more limber, and build more muscle mass. By *weight bearing,* we mean activity that makes your body work against gravity. This "hard" work encourages the various mechanical, electrical, and chemical processes that keep more calcium in the bone tissue and ensure that remodeling continues as it should.

Moderation is the key. It's not necessary to exhaust yourself with a marathon race or a high-impact aerobics class to get the necessary physical benefits you need at this time of life. A brisk two-mile walk each day combined with some easy graded-resistance weight training for the upper body offers protective benefits against osteoporosis. The more varied your exercise program is, the more benefits you'll accrue to your bones.

One of the most important things to remember about physical training is that you have to keep it up in order to maintain the benefits. When you stop exercising, your bone density immediately begins to revert to preexercise levels. And if you don't consistently upgrade your training, either in intensity, frequency, or duration, you won't achieve further increases in bone density. Eventually, everyone will reach a plateau beyond which no more significant gain can be achieved. And for most people, that's fine —as long as they are combining an all-around level of fitness with a good diet and mineral supplementation.

WHAT KIND OF EXERCISE IS MOST BENEFICIAL TO BONE?

Strong bones are essential as you age. But it's even more important to keep the muscles and tendons around those bones flexible and functional to protect and cushion the hard tissue. If you sit or lie down for longer periods of time as you get older, you will lose muscle mass and your tendons will shorten from lack of use. Good muscle tone and tendon flexibility develop only during a regular exercise program.

Some beneficial types of weight-bearing exercise are:

Walking

Jogging

Bicycling

Step training (stair climbing)

Rowing

Low-impact aerobics

Racquet sports

Dancing

Jumprope

Weight training

Swimming—which is a great exercise for people of any age, because it increases cardiovascular health—is not as effective a tool against osteoporosis. When you swim, you aren't bearing your own weight because your body is supported by the water. But a well-rounded exercise program might include two different activities, which you can rotate, and swimming could be one of these.

Other exercise alternatives include dance, yoga, tai chi, and other forms of bodywork such as the Alexander technique and Feldenkrais. These are also excellent methods of taking care of your inner person as you exercise your outer body. (See Chapter 10, "Adjunct Treatments.")

Strength training is also invaluable for bone health, particularly for women who tend to have weaker upper bodies than men. You should start out light—carrying one- or two-pound weights with you as you do your morning walk or filling empty milk bottles with two pounds of sand and doing a few sets of lifts daily. You can stand in front of the television set and raise your arms to your side, circle them, then bend and stretch with them to each side. As the two-pound weights start to feel too easy, upgrade to four-pound weights.

A study at Tufts University on healthy elderly weight trainers showed astounding improvement after only eight weeks. The volunteers, ages 87 to 96, increased their strength 300 to 400 percent by graduated lifting, and two of them, who had relied on canes for walking, found that they no longer needed them!

If you have already been diagnosed with osteoporosis, however, you should not be doing any lifting at all. Consult your physician about any exercise program or combination of activities. High-risk individuals and people with chronic diseases (heart disease, hypertension, cancer, diabetes) should have a diagnostic, physician-supervised stress test before beginning any program.

We can't emphasize enough that exercise—like everything else in life—should be done in moderation. Women who exercise excessively, such as long-distance runners and ballet dancers, have been shown to lose ovarian function. Hormonal output slows or ceases in response to the enormous physical stresses on the body. And since estrogen appears to be one of the most influential factors in women's bone density, *amenorrhea* (absence of menses) places you in a very high risk category for osteoporosis. But young women, still in their reproductive years, who cut back on their excessive exercise regimens and put on some weight—sometimes as little as five pounds—can regain their menses and start to increase bone density again, as long as their estrogen deficiency hasn't gone on longer than three to five years.

TIPS FOR STARTING AND MAINTAINING A REGULAR EXERCISE PROGRAM

In order to protect and maintain your bones, you've got to keep up with your exercise regimen at least half an hour a day, five or six days a week. A program that alternates exercise routines will keep you both flexible and strong.

Always:

1. Get a physician's okay to begin an exercise program.

2. Wear the proper equipment—specifically, good shoes and clothing that breathes.

3. Drink plenty of water, both before and after you exercise.

4. Pick a time of day that's convenient for you; that way you'll be more likely to stick with it.

5. Get expert supervision to start with; an instructor at a health club is ideal.

6. Start slowly and don't overexert yourself; you'll build your stamina and frequency over time.

7. If you feel pain or are short of breath, *stop* exercising; pain often indicates tissue injury, possibly caused by improper technique.

8. *Don't get discouraged* if you feel you aren't making progress and it isn't getting easier. It takes a long time to accustom your body to working out. If you really hate the form of exercise you're doing, try something else. If you find jogging is too lonely a pursuit, switch to a tai chi or low-impact aerobics class.

9. If you need some dramatic motivation, take a look at elderly people who use canes or walkers or are confined to wheelchairs. Your exercise regimen is your insurance policy against dependency and physical immobility in later life.

PREVENTIVE CARE IS THE BEST CARE

When good eating, good supplementation, and good exercise come together, they add up to a well-rounded program that will not only keep you in excellent physical shape but will provide emotional and psychological benefits as well. You can feel good about your future by taking an active role in your own health care.

SIX

LIFE-STYLE CHANGES FOR BETTER BONES

When bone is fragile, it can break at any time. Someone with osteoporosis may simply bend over and fracture a vertebra. Bones can break during a sneeze or cough or a particular movement that puts stress on an already weakened part of the bone. It's for this reason that if you are at high risk for osteoporosis, you are going to have to relearn how to perform "normal activities."

Falling is serious business. Ninety percent of all hip fractures are the result of a fall. And more than one in four individuals over 65 will fall in the next year. If they also suffer from osteoporosis, the fractures they sustain may never heal properly. Fragile, porous bone is less able to withstand blows and knocks than strong, pliable bone and is more likely to break, particularly at the weakest sites—the wrist or forearm, the hip, the vertebrae, or the ribs.

As we age, certain functions we've always relied on begin to decline. Our vision, hearing, and *proprioception* (the ability to feel things with our feet and hands) are less accurate than they used to be. Even the way we move through space is different: We change our gait to get better balance, there's more sway in our walk, and we stand with a broader base than we used to.

Various diseases can also affect our ability to protect ourselves against falls. Cataracts and glaucoma can impair or obliterate vision, whereas degenerative joint disease, arthritis, Parkinson's disease, stroke, and hypotension caused by drugs or other diseases can slow our body's reaction time.

But there is a *great* deal we can do to prevent the accidents that may cause fracture. The preventive tactics we'll outline below are easy, low tech, and no cost or low cost and can possibly save your bones from future injury.

Medical evidence suggests that in many cases of hip fracture you fall because your femur has broken and will no longer support the weight you put on it. In other cases, you may fracture an already weakened bone after falling down. Changing your life-style and taking specific precautionary measures will not change your medical picture but will make your life a lot safer.

PERSONAL CHANGES

1. *Footwear*. Wear only flat, supportive shoes. Give up high heels and slingbacks—also those backless bedroom slippers you just slide your toes into. They all alter your body's alignment, affect balance, and give you uncertain footing on any surface.

Adapt your footwear to your activity. Little stylish flats are not suitable for a walk in the woods where you'll be going over uneven terrain.

Sneakers and walking or running shoes are usually excellent choices for any activity, but try them on a hard surface before purchasing them. Many older people who tend to shuffle feel they have *too* much traction with rubber-soled sneakers, which may stick and cause a fall. Excess traction may also make it difficult to move smoothly across a floor.

2. *Clothing.* Long robes, nightgowns, and coats may prove hazardous to your health, particularly on stairs. If you don't routinely pick up your skirts when you walk, you could trip and fall. To be on the safe side, switch to pajamas and short gowns and robes.

If you have already suffered several vertebral fractures and have a pronounced hump, you will find that your clothes no longer fit the way they used to. Dresses and shirts will be longer in front, for example. There are patterns available from the London School of Design specifically tailored for those with this problem. You may also wish to take a look at the patterns in *Design Without Limits: Designing and Sewing for Special Needs* by Doloris Quinn and Renée Weiss Chase, Drexel Design Press, 1990. Having better-fitting clothes when you have osteoporosis can give you a better self-image and, in fact, make you more determined to stick to your program of eating and increased mobility.

3. *Eyewear.* If you're supposed to wear glasses, wear them! If you wear bifocals, be sure to practice walking downstairs as you look through the top lens for distance vision, never the bottom for close vision. If you wear magnifying glasses just for reading, remember to take them off when you get up and shift your vision far ahead of you. If you haven't been wearing your glasses lately because things look blurry through them, it's time for a checkup and a change of prescription. Some eye specialists now

favor monocular correction for older patients, where one eye is corrected to close vision and the other to distance vision. The brain, amazingly, puts the two together.

4. *Orthopedic devices.* If your doctor has recommended that you walk with a cane, you must get a cane that fits. Different people require different canes. Physical therapists and rehabilitation specialists are experts in evaluating the appropriate device for you at just the right height.

5. *Illness.* Any illness, even a cold, can make us "weak as a kitten" or so fatigued and logy that it's hard to stand up straight. Fever, in particular, can disorient us, acting like a hallucinogenic drug on the body. And alteration in body temperature, going from drenching sweats to teeth-chattering chills, often makes us think that objects are closer or farther away than they actually are.

If you are really ill, make sure you have a friend or relative check on you daily and try to get them to arrange your environment—food, tissues, access to the bathroom —so it's easy for you to manage when you're alone. Don't try to do any physical activity that's not absolutely necessary.

6. *Alcohol, drugs, and medications.* Be aware that alcohol, drugs, and medications all affect your perception, awareness, and balance. If you have osteoporosis, it can be just as dangerous to walk after drinking a glass of wine or taking any mind-affecting drug as it is to drive a car while under the influence.

Many medications can make navigating around the house or even from bedroom to bathroom a mine field of possible disasters. The worst offenders are long-acting sedatives such as Valium, Librium, and Dalmane. These drugs have half-lives of from 36 to 72 hours, and when taken daily, levels build up in the blood. These drugs are all associated with a high risk of hip fracture, since a drugged sleeper may try to get up in the middle of the night to use the bathroom and fall and break a hip. There are many short-acting sedatives you can take that are just as effective and far less hazardous.

Antidepressants, antihistamines, and antipsychotics also have sedating side effects. And antihypertensive and diuretic drugs often cause *orthostatic hypotension*—that dizzy feeling you get when your blood pressure drops if you change position quickly. This often occurs after eating, so it's a good idea to hold on to the dining table as you get up from a meal.

If you have to be on medication, take extra precautions about walking and moving. Cut out or cut down on your consumption of alcohol. And be wary of over-the-counter drugs that may interact with one another or with your prescribed medications to further distort your perception and balance. Discuss all your medications with your physician to see whether some could be reduced or eliminated.

ACTIVITIES, INDOORS

If you have already been diagnosed with osteoporosis, you should not engage in any household activities that involve pushing, pulling, or lifting. If you know that you are at high risk for osteoporosis, you should do these activities only after your physician has given you the go-ahead.

1. *Watching television and reading.* Don't sit on a couch. It's like a big trap—easy to get into, difficult to get out of.

Get a good, straight chair, with arms to use as support when you get up and sit down. Lift chairs, which assist you up and down, are another possibility.

2. *Working at a desk or computer.* Sit with a towel roll or a lumbar back support behind the small of your back. (See Chapter 10, "Adjunct Treatments.") Be sure to get up at regular intervals and stretch.

3. *Vacuuming and sweeping.* Use your legs and lower back for this activity instead of your arms and upper back. As you move the wand or broom across the floor, stay as upright as possible. Don't extend your arms to their fullest measure so that you are reaching for those hard-to-get areas but, rather, walk with the vacuum cleaner or broom to every corner.

4. *Opening a window.* In most cases, if the window is at all difficult to open or if it's situated at an odd angle (on the other side of a counter, shelf, or radiator), get someone else to do this for you. If you have to open it yourself, get close to it—if you have to, climb up on the counter—so that you don't have to reach as you pull up on the sash.

- Stand as close to the window as possible.

- Lift symmetrically (applying the same amount of pressure to both sides at the same time).

- Keep the natural arch in your lower back—that is, don't slouch (which removes all arch) and don't stick out your rear end (which gives too much arch).

- Bend your knees when you lift so that you're using leg and back strength rather than arm strength.

• Don't put your wrists in an end-range position, that is, hand flexed back sharply against the wrist.

5. *Moving furniture.* The first rule of thumb is Don't do it! If you absolutely must, position yourself carefully in back of the piece of furniture, make sure you have proper curve in your back, and use your back and leg muscles— never your arms or upper back—to do the work. Push symmetrically, and don't put your wrists in end-range position.

6. *Sex.* You may have to make certain accommodations in position for sexual intimacy. Big, sturdy cushions on the bed can prop you up—and an understanding partner is important too. Be sure to ask your physician or physical therapist for recommendations. If you can talk openly about this, your health-care provider can too.

ACTIVITIES, OUTDOORS

1. *Taking out the garbage.* Keep garbage bags small and light; don't pack them excessively because you shouldn't lift more than five pounds at any one time. Bend your knees when you stoop to pick up the bag and carry it close to your body, positioned in the center rather than to one side or the other. If you have a lot of large, heavy trash, get one of those garbage can trolleys and simply wheel it to the curb for collection. Don't lift a heavy can under any circumstances.

2. *Shoveling snow.* The best way to do this activity is to hire a young person to shovel your walk for $5! This is one of the most dangerous pursuits for someone who has

osteoporosis or even someone at risk for osteoporosis. If you must shovel snow yourself, use the same principles as for vacuuming, on page 84. Buy a shovel with an angle in the pole to reduce the strain of lifting, and keeping the shovel close to your body, use the strength from your legs and lower back to do the work. Be sure to keep the natural curve in your back as you move.

Never pick up a shovelful of snow to move it—*always* keep the weight on the ground and push it forward. Again, let the energy come up from the base of your spine and direct the push through your arms.

EXERCISES TO ENHANCE YOUR AWARENESS OF WHAT'S AROUND YOU

1. *Learn to feel the floor.* As we get older, our tactile perception declines, and our awareness of where we are in space diminishes—both from the aging process of the nervous system and from a lack of attention to our surroundings. Make a conscious effort, when sitting, standing, or getting up, to feel all the points of your foot gripping the floor. This includes your toe, heel, ball, instep, and sides of the foot. Imagine your foot having roots that go deep through the floor and into the ground. Practice this exercise on a regular basis barefoot and then with your shoes on. You will find that simply by paying attention to the connection of your sole to the ground, your balance has improved.

2. *Get up slowly from a seated or lying position.* Orthostatic imbalance (when you feel dizzy if you get up too fast) is increasingly common as we get older, particularly

after meals. The rapid change of position and the blood rushing to your stomach to aid in digestion both cause your diastolic blood pressure to drop. Many people see spots in front of their eyes and feel as though they're going to faint.

It is essential to spend time relearning how to get up, particularly if you rise from bed in the middle of the night often to go to the bathroom. Do it in stages. Push yourself up on your elbow, and stay there for a moment. Then rise to a sitting position and stay there, with both feet flat on the floor. Stand up, bracing yourself on the bed or sturdy night table and stay there for a moment. Finally, when you feel completely in equilibrium, begin to move.

When getting up from the table after a meal, lean on the table and stay in a standing position until you feel comfortable.

3. *Balance practice.* When we were children, we often tested ourselves, standing or hopping on one leg, whirling around madly and then stopping, trying to stand erect. These exercises can be a profitable part of training the body for better balance as we age.

Start easily, standing with your weight on one leg and with your other leg just lightly touching the floor, and hold the position for half a minute. Then switch legs. Don't overdo this. If you feel dizzy, immediately put your weight on both legs.

When this feels too easy for you, take the foot that's still touching off the floor. This will improve not only your balance but the strength in your *quadriceps* (the large muscle on top of your thigh).

Eventually, try holding the position for a minute and

then for two minutes. Better balance means that even if you do trip, you'll be better able to recover and get yourself upright before you can fall and break a bone.

Correct lifting technique.

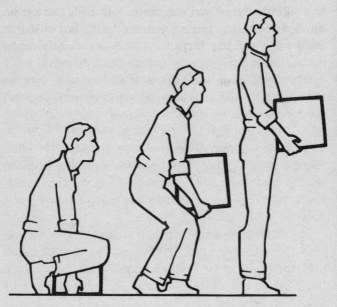

To reduce stress on the lower back, bend your knees, not your back. Keep the object you're carrying close to your body. Heavy objects should be carried at waist height.

4. *Lifting practice.* If you can, keep all lifting under five pounds. Always bend your knees and squat down to pick up a heavy object. Carry it close to your body, positioned in the middle rather than to one side. Practice lifting on a regular basis, even when you don't have to, and it will increase your ability to handle a heavy object.

Although we know it is preferable to ask for paper rather than plastic bags at the supermarket for environmental reasons, it is far safer to carry your groceries in a bag with handles so that you can pick them up with your hands without straining your back. (No matter how you try, the only way to get a paper bag out of your car seat or trunk is to bend at the waist and lug the sack toward you.) The best solution is to purchase canvas bags with handles and *always* keep them in your car when you go shopping.

If your doctor has told you that you absolutely cannot lift or you are unable to bend over from the waist due to arthritis, ask for a referral to an occupational therapist who can provide you with a special device to do the lifting for you.

CHANGING YOUR ENVIRONMENT, INDOORS

1. *Floors.* Do not polish your wood or linoleum floors until you can see your face in them. A highly polished surface is an invitation to slip and skid, and the glare coming off the shining floor may make it difficult for you to see—or even to judge the distance to the floor.

If you have linoleum in your home, check for chipped pieces or areas where the flooring is unglued and lifting. It's easy to trip on a floor that isn't level.

2. *Rugs*. Roll up and put away your throw rugs. Even if they have pads underneath, it's too easy to skid on them. You may love the look of hardwood floors, but it is safer to put down carpeting. Aside from being slipproof, carpets and the padding that's installed below give you an extra cushion in case you do fall.

3. *Stairs*. Whenever you walk downstairs, hold the railing. If you have a runner or carpeting on your stairs, check each riser to be certain that the material is securely tacked down.

4. *Bathrooms*. A tub can be a treacherous surface when wet. Be sure to use a rubber bath mat or traction strips on the tub bottom. When getting out, always hold on to handrails or well-anchored towel bars for security. You might consider having grab bars professionally installed.

5. *Electrical wires*. Secure all electrical wires, tacking them along the baseboards leading to the outlets. Whenever possible, keep lighting fixtures close enough to the outlet so that you don't need extension cords. When doing a quick electrical job or putting up a temporary fixture, like Christmas tree lights, give as much care to their placement as you would if they were to be permanently installed.

6. *Toys*. If you have young children in the house, make a rule that all roller skates and skateboards must be restricted to outdoors. Invoke strict cleanup rules concerning games and other toys with small pieces that somehow always end up underfoot.

7. *Clutter.* If you're in the habit of leaving things around, make a new habit to keep the floors clean of all paraphernalia.

8. *Pets.* If you have small dogs and cats, always look down before you get up from a chair or sofa so that you don't inadvertently step on one. This is really important in the middle of the night when you may get up to go to the bathroom and trip over an unexpected tail or paw.

9. *Bedside arrangement.* Make sure you have a sturdy bedside table you can lean on when you get out of bed. Many hip fractures occur when one is getting out of bed in the middle of the night, half asleep. If you feel uncertain of your footing from bedroom to bathroom, consider keeping a bedpan under your bed.

10. *Nighttime lighting.* You should have excellent lighting from your bedroom down the hallway to the bathroom and on the stairs. Small guidelights that plug into outlets below wall baseboards are usually sufficient, but if they don't provide enough light, snap on extra lights as you go.

CHANGING YOUR ENVIRONMENT, OUTDOORS

1. *Lighting.* The areas around your house should be well lighted at night. A porch or deck light and a light that spills from the driveway to your house can be a bone-saver —if not a lifesaver.

2. *Pavement.* If you have cracked or uneven pavement outside your house, get it fixed professionally. If you live in an apartment, be aware of your surroundings outside and pay attention to trouble spots on streets you often walk.

3. *Road surfaces.* A snowy or icy walk should be sanded or salted, or you can coat it with Kitty Litter. It's best to have someone do this for you so you don't slip while putting it down.

4. *Using the grass.* When in doubt about your footing, walk on the grass even if it's wet and muddy rather than venturing onto the sidewalk or pavement, especially if you can see that it's not sanded or salted.

5. *Sitting in the car.* Always wear seat belts with shoulder harnesses. Even if you have to stop short or swerve around a curve, your back will stay in position when you're strapped in.

6. *Parking the car.* One of the chief hazards of parallel parking is turning to see how much distance you have behind you. This movement requires you to torque your back, leaving your hips facing front as you twist around. In order to park safely, position a mirror on the passenger side of your car. This way, by glancing alternately in the rearview mirror and the passenger-side mirror, you will be able to maneuver the car into position, while keeping your spine in alignment.

KEEP YOURSELF SAFE FOR A LIFETIME
OF GOOD BONES

These preventive tactics are important whether or not you've been diagnosed with osteoporosis. The falls you *don't* have may save you years of disabling pain.

SEVEN

MEDICAL TREATMENTS

Unfortunately, there is no cure for osteoporosis. Once sufficient bone mass and density are lost, and fractures begin, your body will never be able to rebuild new bone to match the former tensile strength of its early years.

However, there are a variety of medical treatments available that will halt the loss of bone density and even occasionally encourage some bone growth. In this chapter, we'll discuss the medications that are currently being used and the experimental programs now under way that may change the nature of osteoporosis treatment in the future.

If you are concerned about developing osteoporosis, or if you currently have osteoporosis, you should discuss all the medical alternatives with your physician and together decide on the right course for you.

HORMONE REPLACEMENT THERAPY

The History of ERT and HRT

In the 1930s at Massachusetts General Hospital, a physician named Dr. Fuller Albright, doing experimentation with pigeons that were about to lay eggs, discovered how vital estrogen is to bone formation. As the pigeons prepared to lay and their hormone levels rose, osteoblastic activity increased and their bones became stronger, less prone to fracture. Albright later noted that women who had their ovaries surgically removed during their reproductive years—cutting off their estrogen source much sooner than normal—were likely to develop osteoporosis much earlier than women who went through natural menopause.

His seminal work on estrogen and bone strength led to many subsequent studies on supplemental estrogen. As ERT (estrogen replacement therapy) became popular in the 1970s for relief of menopausal symptoms, it was also discovered that bone density increased in women who were taking supplemental hormones.

By 1975, estrogen was among the top ten drugs prescribed in the United States. Dr. Robert A. Wilson was its chief proponent, claiming that ERT was a "fountain of youth" for women. Not only would it strengthen their bones, but it would protect their cardiovascular systems, renew their sex lives, and restore that youthful "glow." He gave his patients large doses of unopposed estrogen (that is, without progesterone) just before menopause and suggested they continue taking the medication indefinitely.

But that same year, several independent research teams denounced estrogen for use longer than one year as a cause of endometrial cancer. Since the postmenopausal body doesn't produce progesterone, the lining of the uterus would not slough off each month in a menstrual period. In a small percentage of patients, this thickened lining could become cancerous. Newer forms of hormone replacement therapy (HRT) were then devised so that not just estrogen but also progesterone would be supplemented, and women taking the regimen would have a "period" each month as the lining of the uterus sloughed off.

For the past two decades, a great deal of research, experimentation, and controversy have swirled around HRT. The progestin portion of the regimen, particularly, has come under scrutiny. Though it somewhat mitigates the cardiovascular benefit (see page 101) you receive from estrogen, it is highly beneficial to bone tissue. It may, however, cause a variety of side effects, including mood changes, bloating, breast tenderness, and depression. And what woman over age 50 really wants to have a period?

Despite its drawbacks, the general medical consensus is that all women who have an intact uterus (and therefore a uterine lining) should take both estrogen and progesterone (HRT). Women with no uterus (hysterectomized) and/ or no ovaries (oophorectomized) need only take estrogen (ERT). Even newer designations, though not widely in use, are *ET* for "estrogen therapy" and *CHT* for "combined hormone therapy."

HRT and Osteoporosis

Both ERT and HRT—taken orally, or by transdermal patch, percutaneous gel, or subcutaneous implant—are equally effective against bone loss. Not every woman's body responds to estrogen, however. Through some bio-chemical failure not well understood, roughly 10 percent see no benefit from supplemental hormones whatsoever. And there are certain contraindications (see pages 108–109) to hormone use, depending on your medical history. However, hormone therapy is the most widely recom-mended avenue of prevention and method of treatment for osteoporosis.

Between one third and one half of women with estab-lished osteoporosis who seek treatment are put on HRT. When the body's estrogen level is boosted synthetically after menopause, the body is once again able to retain calcium in the bones. This effectively prevents further bone loss and reduces risk of fracture by 75 percent (ver-tebral) and 50 percent (hip). Studies done on long-term HRT—that is, ten years—show that replacement therapy reduces vertebral fracture frequency by 90 percent. It doesn't even matter how old you are when you begin; the treatment has been shown to halt bone loss in elderly patients as well. Its effect on the fracture rate in older people is not yet known.

Estrogen will restore the balance of bone resorption and re-formation (see Chapter 1). But in women who are past their peak bone mass years, it is unlikely that even estrogen—in combination with calcium supplements and weight-bearing exercise—can restore any significant amount of mass or density. Some studies have shown that elderly women who have lost a great deal of density can regain a small amount when they begin HRT, but basi-cally, once bone is gone, it's gone—and that's what occurs in the normal process of aging. However, taking estrogen can *slow* bone loss, helping you retain the bone density you currently have and preventing further loss. It can make the difference between the normal aging process of bone over several decades and osteoporosis.

Length of Therapy

Estrogen replacement is only protective to your bones as long as you take it. If you stop, your bone mass will immediately start to decrease.

Many physicians currently recommend that you begin replacement therapy no more than two years after your menopause and continue at least to age 70, when your body will probably have readjusted to its new hormonal levels. Most of your bone loss takes place in the five to ten years following your menopause. It goes without saying that the sooner you begin the therapy, the better your chances of forestalling bone loss.

Having a bone densitometry test around the time of your menopause will give you and your physician an opportunity to evaluate your bone profile. (See Chapter 4.) Once you have learned how much bone you've lost, you can decide—with your physician—whether you need to start HRT at that point or should wait a year or so and be tested again.

If you do start therapy, you should review your decision to continue with your physician each year. It's a good idea to do a second densitometry test to see how you're responding to the estrogen—whether you're gaining bone, maintaining or losing at a slower rate. Your physician may decide to alter your dosage, depending on your situation.

If you should decide to stop HRT because of your possible concerns about long-term risks, about costs, or for any other reason, be sure to do it in consultation with your physician. Abrupt withdrawal of the replacement hormones can start up a variety of menopausal discomforts such as hot flashes and vaginal dryness.

How Will You Take ERT or HRT?

There is a variety of routes of administration for these supplements, and all are equally effective against osteoporosis.

1. *Oral administration, cyclical.* A low dose of estrogen (0.625 mg Premarin or another conjugated estrogen) is given for the first 25 days of what will become your "cycle." A progestin (5 mg Provera, a trade name for medroxyprogesterone) is added for days 12 to 25 if you have a uterus. You will take no supplements for the remainder of the month and will then have a "period."

2. *Oral administration, continuous.* A low dose of both estrogen and progestin is given daily. After the first three months, when you may see some spotting, you should have no breakthrough bleeding.

Oral HRT is the method preferred by most physicians for protection against osteoporosis. Estrogen changes blood lipid levels when taken orally, and it boosts the HDL (high-density lipoprotein—"good") cholesterol—both of these are preventive factors against coronary heart disease. But estrogen taken orally passes through the digestive system and must be processed by the liver. Overstimulation of certain liver proteins has been shown to create benign tumors in some women.

Women who have undergone surgical menopause (oophorectomy) tend to lose more bone density more quickly and do best with the oral dosage. (See Chapter 9.)

3. *Transdermal patch.* A patch with an estrogen reservoir is applied to the hip or buttock after swabbing the area with alcohol. The skin is the semipermeable membrane through which the estrogen enters the body. The patch is changed twice a week. It contains continuous (28-day) estradiol-17-beta, 0.05 mg or 0.1 mg daily, in combination with an oral dosage of a progestin called norethisterone acetate (0.25 mg daily for 14 of each 28 days).

The advantage of the patch is that it bypasses the liver. Some doctors highly favor the patch; others feel it doesn't give enough cardiac protection because it doesn't promote the same lipid changes as the oral medication.

Studies have shown, however, that if the patient is thorough and consistent with the reapplication of the patch, this dosage is as effective as the oral dosage in preventing bone loss from the spine and hip in women who have undergone a natural menopause.

4. *Percutaneous gel.* This estrogen gel dries into a patch. Same administration as number 3, above. The gel will not cause the same skin irritation as the patch; however, dosage is not as consistent.

5. *Subcutaneous implant.* A small estrogen pellet is implanted in the lower abdomen and can be safely left there for anywhere from three months to a year before it's changed. Some experimental studies have used a Progestasert IUD (intrauterine device) for the progestin portion of the regimen.

In women with no uterus, the progestin is omitted.

How Does Estrogen Work on Bone Tissue?

Researchers aren't exactly sure why estrogen is so beneficial to bone. It's clear that it inhibits bone resorption, but this isn't the only helpful factor. There appear to be special estrogen *receptor sites*—something like open doorways that only let in this particular hormone—in the osteoblasts. There may also be an insulinlike growth factor that helps the estrogen work on these cells. Another theory is that estrogen and 1,25-hydroxyvitamin D_3 may stimulate production of endogenous calcitonin, one of the hormones involved in the maintenance of bone mass.

HRT and Heart Disease

The benefits of HRT go beyond good bone maintenance in your later years, as has been clearly shown in study after study, most particularly the now-famous ten-year survey of over 48,000 nurses who were monitored by physicians at Brigham and Women's Hospital. The results were reported in 1991 in the *New England Journal of Medicine*. This survey gave new reason to trust in the benefits of estrogen after menopause, indicating that women who take the hormone can cut their risk of heart attack in half. Adding a progestin, for those women with an intact uterus, somewhat decreases the good effect—HRT is about half as effective as ERT in increasing the HDLs in the blood. This is still a better percentage than having no hormone at all in your system. Since heart disease is the leading cause of death in women, taking more lives than all combined cancers, this is another persuasive reason to consider hormone replacement therapy.

During the reproductive years, women tend to contract

cardiovascular disease six times less frequently than men. Possibly because estrogen keeps artery walls free of plaque, women tend to have more "good" HDL cholesterol and fewer heart attacks than men before they go through menopause. It's also thought that women who have children have wider coronary arteries that accommodated for the increased blood pumping during childbirth. Young women's blood vessels also tend to be more elastic than men's and seem to be able to repair any damage done by moderate hypertension.

But after 50, the picture for women changes drastically. During the 15 to 20 years after menopause, a woman is 30 times more likely than before menopause to contract coronary artery disease. Heart disease in women has been so neglected in research and clinical medicine that doctors tend to ignore the symptoms that would have them rush a man in for cardiac catheterization or a bypass. And since some female symptoms are different from male symptoms, many doctors are unprepared to treat them adequately.

HRT has been highly touted as a preventive treatment for all menopausal women who have no contraindications (see below for a discussion of cancer risks). Those with a family history of heart disease should discuss the options for HRT with their physician. The kind of protection that estrogen offers to the heart and arteries is even more significant as you grow older.

Risk of Endometrial Cancer

The overall lifetime risk of developing endometrial cancer is 1 in 1,000. (Compare this, if you will, with an overall lifetime risk of 31 percent for women developing any form of cardiovascular disease.) This cancer can appear if the endometrium, or lining of your uterus, becomes over-stimulated by estrogen, which may conceivably occur on a hormone replacement regimen.

As estrogen is supplied to the endometrium, the lining begins to grow new cells. This is the normal monthly course of events. But intense stimulation by estrogen may cause the glands in the uterine lining to increase in number and become more irregular in shape. Over time, this overgrowth, or *hyperplasia,* can become premalignant.

Every woman's body is different and responds differently to medication. Even on a continuous oral dosage, most women have some withdrawal bleeding for the first few months. However, if you begin to bleed in an irregular or abnormal manner, your doctor will undoubtedly want to do an *endometrial biopsy,* where he or she removes a small clump of cells from the endometrium for examination at a pathology lab. This is an office procedure that is sometimes performed even before you are put on hormone therapy.

Irregular bleeding can be one of the first signs of endometrial overgrowth. A biopsy will tell the physician whether this bleeding is simply a sign of your system slowing down or whether cancer should be suspected.

The method of dosage can be very important here. Since most women over 50 don't want to be bothered with periods anymore, most will only continue with a hormone regimen with which they don't bleed. Physicians have found that continuous HRT medication usually eliminates a period, and some have tried giving progestin only once every two or three months to cut down on the number of periods a year. However, after only 17 weeks of supplying estrogen without progesterone to the uterus, hyperplasia can result. This condition is treatable: *cystic* and *simple adenomatous hyperplasia* are not cancerous and are often treated with hormone (progestin) therapy. *Atypical adenomatous hyperplasia,* the premalignant state, can be treated with surgery.

This stage I cancer is not considered a contraindication to continuing hormone therapy. Endometrial cancer is slow growing and is relatively simple to treat in its early stages. And because of the protective effect of the progestin given in the second half of the therapy cycle, some short-term (five-year) studies report that the risk of endometrial cancer is *lower* in women on HRT than in women on no therapy at all.

As yet there are no studies available on women who've been on HRT for more than ten years; so it remains to be seen how prolonged exposure to replacement hormones will affect a woman's chances of developing endometrial cancer.

Breast Cancer and Fibrocystic Breast Disease

If you are a healthy woman concerned with the statistic that there is a one in nine lifetime risk that you may develop breast cancer, should you consider hormone replacement therapy? Breast cancer kills 43,000 American women a year, and the numbers of those who develop the disease are alarmingly on the rise.

In August 1989, the *New England Journal of Medicine* published a report on a five-year Swedish study. The researchers had been monitoring the effects of using a combination of estrogen and a progestin to relieve menopausal symptoms. The results were distressingly negative about the possibility of HRT reducing the risk of breast cancer.

Of the 23,244 women in the study, one third took no hormones at all; one third were on estrogen therapy only; and the final third took both hormones. The rate of breast cancer in the last group was four times as high as the rate among women who took no hormones at all and twice as high as those who only took estrogen. Of the total number, 253 women developed breast cancer during the years of the study.

Because the estrogen used in the Swedish study was not the type or dosage of conjugated estrogen prescribed in America, researchers have since downplayed the global implications of this study. Since that time, there have been dozens of other reports on the opposite side of the argument. An Australian *meta-analysis* (that is, a statistical survey of many studies combined together) of 23 studies of estrogen use and breast cancer concluded that estrogen did not alter the risk of a woman's contracting breast cancer. A Centers for Disease Control meta-analysis showed no increased risk in the first 5 years of HRT use but a 30 percent increase in risk after 15 years of use. None of the studies indicate any difference in risk between ERT and HRT.

The biggest determinant of risk, in any of these studies, seems to be the *dosage*. Patients who use higher than 0.625 mg daily of conjugated estrogen or who receive estrogen by injection or in pellet form might be at greater risk for breast cancer. It is worth mentioning that the mortality rate is about the same for women with breast cancer who have been on hormone therapy as it is for women with breast cancer who have never been on hormone therapy.

A great deal more investigation must be done before anyone can say for certain how HRT may contribute to the development of breast cancer. It goes without saying, however, that if you have been diagnosed with estrogen-dependent breast cancer during your reproductive years, you *should not* be on HRT in any form. You and your doctor will have to discuss other risk factors such as a family history of breast cancer. Each woman is different, and each case has to be assessed individually.

If you have fibrocystic breasts, you're not necessarily at risk for breast cancer, though it can be difficult to tell one disease from another in their early stages. HRT is not absolutely out of the question for you if you tend to have cystic breasts, as long as you are on the continuous oral regimen. (The cysts proliferate with fluctuating, rather than steady, hormone levels.) Some studies have shown great reduction in fibrocystic breast disease simply by removing *all* caffeine from the diet for six months and then keeping caffeine intake extremely low thereafter. You should discuss this possibility with your physician.

How Do I Decide Whether Hormone Replacement Therapy Is for Me?

The medical controversy over whether or not women should take replacement hormones to make up for the decline in estrogen that occurs naturally after menopause has been widely publicized. And as with all issues that relate to our health, safety, and long life, there is no right answer.

The questions you must ask yourself are:

1. Do the benefits of taking hormones outweigh the risks, some of which are unknown?

2. Can you live with the uncertainty of what may happen to you 15 or 20 years down the line? (The longest available studies are only of ten years' duration.)

3. Are there certain unknown risks you prefer to others? For example, some people would rather risk a heart attack than any form of cancer.

4. Does taking supplementation conform to your own personal beliefs about following the natural dictates of your body?

Your own answer as to what is right for you must be based on the information you have, your physician's opinion, and your own needs.

Currently, only about 10 percent of postmenopausal women in the United States are taking hormones, though most obstetrician/gynecologists recommend therapy for women who have never had an estrogen-dependent cancer, a history of blood clots, sickle cell anemia, varicose veins, or kidney or liver disease. The treatment costs about $100 to $200 a year, which is not reimbursed by most insurance plans.

Liver and Gallbladder Risks

As was mentioned before, oral estrogen goes through the digestive system and must be processed by the liver. This can overstimulate the liver and seems to affect the production of certain liver proteins. Benign liver tumors have been seen in women on HRT.

The gallbladder, too, can be overstimulated by estrogen and tends to thicken the bile produced by the liver. Surgery for removal of gallstones is two to three times more prevalent in women on HRT.

Other Contraindications to HRT

Smoking cigarettes is bad for your health. It causes lung problems and weakens bone tissue; it also interacts with estrogen to change blood-clotting patterns and increases the risk of *thrombophlebitis* (severe inflammation of a vein that may send a life-threatening embolism to the lung).

Estrogen and progesterone tend to promote fluid retention in the body. You would have to be monitored carefully on an HRT regimen if you are prone to asthma, migraine headaches, epilepsy, or cardiac or kidney disease, all of which are exacerbated by excess fluid.

In rare cases, estrogen use can raise blood pressure. If you're on HRT, you should have your pressure checked on a regular basis.

Contraindications to HRT: Summary

If you have had or currently have *breast cancer,* you should *never* be on HRT.

The following conditions are contraindications to taking supplemental hormones, but each individual case is different. You should discuss the options with your physician:

Gallstones

Kidney or liver disease

Varicose veins

History of blood clots or stroke

Sickle cell anemia

Deep vein thrombosis

Pulmonary blockage

You are at slight risk if you have a history of any of the following conditions:

Other estrogen-related disease (endometriosis, fibroid tumors)

High blood pressure

Diabetes

Obesity

Migraine headaches

If HRT Is Not Right for *You*

If you don't wish to take hormones or cannot because of family history or another disease process but you do have a high osteoporosis profile, there are several other alternative treatments your physician can discuss with you.

OTHER ANTIRESORPTIVE DRUGS

Calcitonin

Calcitonin is a hormone that blocks bone resorption. We don't have a great amount of it circulating in the bloodstream naturally, but in large amounts, this hormone can act as a drug. This medication, Food and Drug Administration (FDA) approved for the treatment of osteoporosis, is currently available only in injectable form. It is made from synthetic hormones designed to resemble the calcitonin produced in salmon. The drug seems to inhibit osteoclast function—like estrogen, it slows bone resorption. Women who have decided against HRT or who cannot take estrogen take this hormone daily, every other day, or three times a week, depending on their bodies' needs. While the therapy appears to be effective, it is very costly (about $1,280 per year) but may be covered by some forms of insurance.

This type of hormone is inactivated by stomach acid, so you can't take it in pill form. Currently, one of the major problems with this drug is that you must learn to give yourself an intramuscular injection or have someone do it for you. The drug should be approved by the FDA in a nasal spray form within the next two years. There are currently forty-two experimental clinical trials ongoing in the United States for this nasal spray, and it is already in use in sixty other countries around the world. When this product comes on the American market, calcitonin will certainly be more widely used in osteoporosis therapy.

An additional benefit of calcitonin, aside from slowing the progress of bone loss, is that it appears to have a pain-reducing effect. The analgesic effect will be more pronounced in the nasal spray form, because the drug will speed directly to the brain through the olfactory glands.

Nausea is a common side effect. Although this reaction can diminish over time, many patients have to take an antinausea drug following their injection. Another alternative is to take the drug just prior to going to sleep. Some patients on long-term calcitonin therapy develop antibodies to the drug and start to show redness, irritation, and swelling at the injection site.

There is, unfortunately, little known about how calcitonin affects fracture rates. It clearly stabilizes bone density and even encourages some increase in bone density, but it's too soon to say how protective it will ultimately be against fractures.

Doctors have yet to explore the full possibilities of calcitonin, but as the nasal spray comes into use, more studies will be done on the efficacy of this drug for osteoporosis treatment.

Bisphosphonates

Etidronate is the most widely tested of the family of drugs known as bisphosphonates. These drugs are currently being used in trials—and are not yet available to the general public.

Like estrogen, etidronate inhibits bone resorption by slowing down the action of the osteoclasts. Etidronate is taken orally, and it travels through the bloodstream to bind to the bone. Its effectiveness lies in its propensity for linking with bone; its drawback is that it has a poor oral absorption rate (a drawback common to all the bisphosphonates).

Originally, etidronate functioned as a water softener on

ships in the navy. Since it binds to calcium, it was used to take the scale off the inside of the boilers. With this auspicious beginning, scientists began to examine its potential for use with the calcium in the human body.

This drug is not yet FDA approved for osteoporosis, although it has been in general use for Paget's disease for many years. Currently, a four-year trial of the drug for osteoporosis is being evaluated, but the results are not yet in. The first two years of the study indicated slight increases in bone density and a lower fracture rate. Then, in the third year, the fracture rate increased slightly. The fourth-year statistics are better, but most doctors feel that if the FDA does approve etidronate, it will be for short-term use only. The other problem with this drug is that it increases bone density inconsistently throughout the body—increasing trabecular bone in the spine but failing to do so in the hip and in the cortical bone of the wrist. An additional complication is compliance with a difficult dosage schedule: Oral etidronate must be taken on an empty stomach, one hour before a meal or two hours after. It is also cycled—two weeks on and two and a half weeks off.

Etidronate is the least potent of the bisphosphonates and probably the least effective for osteoporosis.

Other members of this family are *alendronate, pamidronate, tiludronate,* and *risidronate.* (The last two are currently in the clinical trial stage.) At the moment, pamidronate (ten times as potent as etidronate) is given only intravenously as treatment for a bone malignancy known as hypercalcemia and is also prescribed for treatment of Paget's disease.

Alendronate (100 times as potent as etidronate) is currently nearing the end of its clinical trial period in oral form. Since it is such a potent drug, researchers are anxious to find the minimum amount required to encourage bone growth without side effects. They also wish to see how the drug affects fracture rates in all age-groups with all types of bone loss.

STIMULATORS OF BONE FORMATION

In all the therapies mentioned, the goal is to inhibit bone resorption. However, another tactic is to stimulate bone formation. Up until a few years ago, a promising method of stimulating the osteoblasts was to give supplemental doses of *sodium fluoride* to menopausal women.

Scientists began experimenting with this treatment for bone tissue after it was clearly proven that supplemental sodium fluoride in the drinking water made teeth stronger and reduced cavities. Bone tissue, like your teeth, may be stimulated by fluoride treatment, particularly in the presence of estrogen. Yet there is no definitive proof that living in an area with treated water makes you less vulnerable to osteoporosis in later life.

Fluoride increases trabecular bone density, but at the same time, it decreases cortical bone density, so the resulting bone is fragile: It has more mass but is of low quality. High doses of rapidly absorbed fluoride caused new bone tissue that fractured easily, which is why its use has been downplayed. This treatment can also cause many unpleasant side effects such as nausea, vomiting, and aching joints.

Currently, the jury is still out on the efficacy of fluoride treatment. It is no longer being used in America, although it is commonly prescribed in Europe at much lower dosages than the ones in the U.S. trials. But a number of growth factors have been found in bone from research with fluoride and are being studied for their possible use in healing fractures and stimulating new bone growth in osteoporosis patients.

Anabolic steroids, the steroids some athletes use to build muscle, can increase bone mass. Prolonged use of steroids is dangerous in women because of its masculinizing tendencies. It also causes fluid retention and has adverse effects on carbohydrate and lipid levels and on liver function. They have been prescribed by some doctors for osteoporosis treatment, but because of the possible dangers, they are out of favor with most of the medical profession.

Parathyroid hormone is still in the testing stage, but many researchers feel it is promising, since it increases total bone mass.

Calcitriol is the activated form of vitamin D (1,25-dihydroxyvitamin D_3). This hormone greatly improves calcium absorption from the intestine and enhances its availability to bone. The osteoblasts themselves contain receptors for calcitriol, which means that the hormone could have a direct effect on bone formation. Some studies showed that it reduced fracture risk, whereas others seemed to negate that claim.

Calcitriol's main problem as a drug of choice is that it produces potentially toxic side effects at high doses: kidney stones, calcification of the kidney tubules, renal failure, and high blood and urinary levels of calcium. The dosage that has been used in research is 0.25 mg once or twice a day.

Calcitriol use requires careful monitoring by the physician. Blood and urine levels must be checked every two months, and extreme care must be taken about diet. If you suddenly happened to increase your calcium intake, you could become dangerously hypercalcemic—which could adversely affect your brain function.

The medication is appropriate for a very responsible patient with advanced osteoporosis who can't tolerate estrogen or calcitonin. It is currently available only if you are in a clinical trial program.

Other metabolites of vitamin D are now under investigation and may prove to be easier to take and less risky than calcitriol.

Tamoxifen

This synthetic hormone, used in breast cancer therapy, is —oddly enough—an antiestrogenic drug; that is, it blocks the effect of estrogen in the breast. Animal studies on tamoxifen showed that it acts like estrogen in the body: It reduces bone resorption and turnover, stimulates bone formation, and prevents bone loss after oophorectomy (removal of the ovaries).

Doctors aren't sure why it encourages the growth of trabecular bone in women without much endogenous estrogen, but an interesting new study showed that bone density of the lumbar spine increased in postmenopausal women treated with the drug for breast cancer. The effect on fracture risk is yet to be seen, but tamoxifen seems to have definite possibilities for the future. Its side effects include hot flashes, nausea, and vomiting.

MINERALS AND VITAMINS

Calcium and Vitamin D Supplementation

If you cannot take any medication to treat osteoporosis, or choose not to, your physician will probably recommend mineral and vitamin supplementation as alternative treatments. Vitamins and minerals are not drugs; however, they can correct dietary deficiencies and make a real difference in your bone profile.

In the treatment of osteoporosis, *calcium* and *vitamin D* are essential. No matter how much calcium-rich food we ingest, our intestine only absorbs a certain portion of it, and we excrete a great deal of it in our urine and feces. And as we get older, we absorb less and excrete more.

It's for this reason that postmenopausal women are encouraged to take 1,200 to 1,500 mg of *calcium citrate* or *calcium carbonate* daily. These should be taken with meals to increase absorption. Some physicians recommend oyster shell calcium, and some suggest Tums to their patients as calcium supplements. Tums are a good source of calcium carbonate and are less expensive than citrate. Because Tums are chewable, some patients find it easier to take a daily dose this way.

A multivitamin generally gives you all the *vitamin D* you need (400 IU daily), but if you are elderly, or if you don't get outside much in the winter and early spring, you may have a seasonal D deficiency. Research has shown that more bone loss occurs at this time of the year than at any other.

Those who have had any medical problems or surgical procedures that interfere with absorption, such as gastrectomies for ulcers, small bowel resections, liver disease (where the body can't metabolize 1,25-hydroxyvitamin D_3), renal disease, or malabsorption syndromes like Crohn's disease, should take 800 mg of vitamin D, twice the dose contained in a multivitamin. This is also true for anyone on a long-term antiseizure medication such as Dilantin (phenytoin) and Luminal (phenobarbital), which induce liver enzymes to break down many chemicals, including D, much faster.

In its active forms of 1,25-dihydroxyvitamin D_3 and 1-alpha-hydroxyvitamin D, vitamin D seems to reduce fracture rates, particularly in the elderly. In a new study just reported in France, elderly women in a chronic-care institution suffered far fewer fractures—particularly hip fractures—after several months of ordinary vitamin D supplements and calcium.

Additional Supplementation

Other vitamins that seem to be beneficial in retaining calcium in the bone are *vitamin B_6*, found in whole grain foods and fortified cereals, and *vitamin B_{12}*, found in calves' liver. *Zinc* is a mineral that should also be considered as part of a well-rounded dietary supplement. It can be found in fish and seafood.

You should not be taking supplemental calcium and vitamin D if you are on any of the vitamin D analogs, such as calcitriol. Because of its toxic side effects at high doses, it would be inadvisable to take these minerals in addition to the drug.

MAKING AN INFORMED DECISION ON OSTEOPOROSIS TREATMENTS

How do you know which course of treatment is right for *you*?

The success of any course of medical treatment, in large part, depends on the patient. HRT is not always acceptable to an elderly patient who is unused to taking daily medication—particularly a cyclical form of medication where she must select one drug one day, and another the next—and being closely monitored by a physician. In addition, there are some people who would rather fall and break a bone than take a medication that may increase their risk of getting cancer.

On the other hand, a medication that involves giving yourself a daily injection is also difficult for many. Once calcitonin's nasal spray form receives clearance from the FDA, this may no longer be a problem.

The bisphosphonates are still unavailable unless you are in a clinical trial program, but doctors are hopeful about their prospects since they are medications that have affinity only for bone. They are not systemic—unlike estrogen, which affects bone and many other organs as well.

All the other possibilities for treatment are still in the testing stage.

Each case of osteoporosis is different because there are so many factors that act on one another in this very complex disease. It's for this reason that you must have a physician who really understands the disease and your own prognosis. Only when you have a full grasp of your situation will you be able to weigh all the options—physical and emotional—before making an informed choice on any medical treatments.

EIGHT

OSTEOPOROSIS IN
THE ELDERLY

Although many women weather the postmenopausal period without much decrease in bone mass, the aging process usually takes its toll by the time they reach 75 or 80. They may suddenly sustain a rash of fractures as both trabecular and cortical bone thin out simultaneously. But osteoporosis in the elderly has more consequences than just physical pain and deformity; It can affect a person's entire outlook on life and often restrict or cut off options for social and emotional contact with others.

Nearly half of all men and women over age 75 will break a hip or fracture a vertebra; both cortical and trabecular bone fracture easily in an elderly body with low bone mass. And 12 to 20 percent of patients with hip fractures die within one year of the injury. Those who do survive may be permanently disabled and have to rely on others for the simplest acts of daily life maintenance.

Thanks to better preventive health tactics, advanced medical care, and high-tech surgical innovation, our life expectancy has increased in the past few decades. This does not mean, however, that we are living better as we live longer. The aging process happens to everyone; but as we get older, degenerative diseases often accompany the decline of the immune system. Osteoporosis is an example of a disease that can be difficult to treat if it sets in when the body is already in a deteriorated condition.

HOW MANY GERIATRIC CASES OF OSTEOPOROSIS ARE THERE?

The majority of white and Asian women over age 70 have osteoporosis; 75 percent have vertebral compressions, and by age 90, 33 percent of white women will fracture a hip, and 20 percent of men will fracture one. The incidence goes up exponentially with increasing age because falls are increasingly common owing to medication, bad balance, and reduced reflexes and sensory awareness. Because bone density decreases with advanced age, elderly bodies are more prone to fracture when they fall than younger, more elastic bodies.

The question, then, is not how prevalent osteoporosis is in this group—that's already been well established. The question is how actively physicians should treat the condition in a person over 75.

Most rapid bone loss takes place in the five to ten years after menopause in women. Then a new hormonal balance often establishes itself in the body, and the loss becomes much slower, sometimes stabilizing itself. Some people may actually gain some bone density, depending on changes in nutrition and exercise over time and the ability of the aging intestine to absorb vitamins and minerals. The variations in bone turnover may depend on illness, bed rest, and the kind of diet we're able to maintain. For many older people, calcium supplements and a daily multivitamin—in addition to excellent nutrition—may be all that are necessary to slow the process of further bone loss, even if they already have osteoporosis.

The criterion for going to a physician, or taking an elderly parent to a physician, is the severity of bone loss. How much at risk is your parent, for example, for breaking a hip and being confined to bed or a wheelchair? Are you around to assume responsibility for her meals, her toileting, her bathing?

Remember, even if her physician recommends estrogen replacement or calcitonin, she will not see a significant change in bone density. Perhaps the most the medication will do is prevent a further loss of bone density. But keeping the bone density stable may mean preventing further fractures. Bone grows slowly at any age, but at 75, the rate of turnover is exceptionally slow. If you're lucky, there may be some bone gain after about two or three years of medical treatment. This is, of course, in addition to doing everything possible to prevent falls that might increase the risk of fracture.

WHAT DO THE ELDERLY WHO HAVE OSTEOPOROSIS REALLY NEED?

The most important elements in managing osteoporosis in an older population are:

- A well-rounded diet, high in calcium

- Calcium and vitamin D supplementation

- A daily exercise program that needs no supervision and can be carried out at home by the individual

- A daily dose of sunshine; aside from supplying needed vitamin D, getting outdoors every day is a goal that keeps spirits from flagging

- A group activity; any kind of social interaction will keep an individual functional and more aware of his or her environment—an important challenge to those who spend a lot of time alone

DIET

Many older people who live alone stop caring about what they eat or when they eat it. Those who have lost a spouse with whom they always shared companionable meals may simply feel it's not worth the bother to shop, cook, and sit down to a table by themselves three times a day.

They may grab convenience foods whenever they think of it, and these are often foods low in the nutrients they need. Many elderly people are lactose intolerant and exclude milk and milk products from their diet. This deprives them of calcium and vitamin D, and if they aren't getting out in the sun, either due to weather or lack of motivation, they may be severely deficient in these vitamins and minerals.

Another typical dietary problem is that many medications dull the taste buds. Sweet or salty foods are often preferred. And if nothing seems appetizing, the person may actually become malnourished from not eating regularly.

Alcohol and drugs may cause other problems that interfere with proper diet and absorption of nutrients in the elderly. Antihypertensives compromise the potassium and magnesium status of the body; antibiotics interfere with proper intestinal absorption; laxative use causes cramps and gas and may affect appetite; excess caffeine decreases the body's ability to absorb iron and calcium.

HOW CAN I GET MY PARENT TO EAT A BALANCED DIET?

One solution is to make sure that you or your elderly parent have a reason to prepare or eat meals with others as often as possible. Perhaps there's a friend in your mother's building or down the street with whom she could share shopping and cooking preparations.

There are also Meals on Wheels programs available in most cities and towns, some sponsored by churches, others by the local administration. Senior citizen centers often provide hot lunches, prepared by nutritionists aware of the special needs of older people.

EXERCISE

We know that a daily walking program stresses bone and keeps it vital. Walking involves getting up and out, and for older people, this can be the goal of their entire day. You can walk alone and see the world going on around you, or you can have a walking date with a friend or friends.

Many physicians prescribe a course of physical therapy for a person with osteoporosis who has become dysfunctional or is having difficulty moving. This can be a wonderful intervention for many people, but the problem is that physical therapy generally lasts only two months, and the patient is then left to do her exercises on her own.

For this reason, ask the therapist working with you or

your parent for a daily exercise regimen that can be done alone. Keeping it going is absolutely essential: All benefit will be lost as soon as the activity stops. *Use it, or lose it!* To be effective at any age—but particularly over 75—exercise has to be easy, enjoyable, and done every single day.

A therapist must be given a prescription from the physician appropriate to the special needs of the older osteoporosis patient. He or she should teach the person how to stand, sit, and lie properly; how to change position; and how to lift. (See Chapter 10, "Adjunct Treatments.") The therapist should show the patient how to do gentle muscle-strengthening exercises and, if possible, graded-resistance light weight training with common household objects, so that this activity can be continued even after the therapy ends.

Clearly, the better your physical condition, the more functional you can be around your house and the better protected you are from falling.

RECOVERY AFTER HIP FRACTURE

If you or your elderly parent does break a hip, the most important thing is to restore functional independence as soon as possible. To be independent means being able to get out of bed, go to the bathroom, dress unaided, brew a cup of herb tea, microwave some broccoli, or make a cheese sandwich.

Assuming that you have gone through surgery to have a pin placed in your hip, you will need some time in the hospital to get over the effects of the anesthesia and pain medications. You'll also require time to feel more at home in your repaired body.

Physical problems a patient may incur during a hospital stay include:

- *Immobilization.* Bed sores can result. Obviously, as soon as the patient is ready, he or she should be moved, turned, and encouraged to sit up.

- *Respiratory problems.* Anesthesia may compromise the lungs, and the patient may contract bronchitis, pneumonia, asthma, or emphysema. Use of a bronchodilator can help initially after surgery, and easy breathing exercises can be taught to the patient by a physical therapist.

- *Medication.* A sedated patient is in danger of becoming confused, even delirious. Since elderly patients are usually more susceptible to drug effects than younger patients, it's important that all medication—except pain medication essential to allow the patient to feel comfortable—be kept to a minimum.

- *Heart problems.* It's not uncommon that a patient may have suffered a mild heart attack and fallen as a result —fracturing a hip. For this reason, cardiac monitoring in the hospital after a hip fracture is essential.

- *Constipation or diarrhea.* Either gastrointestinal problem may result after surgery from medication, inactivity, and an erratic diet.

Obviously, you're going to need some help when you get home, and you'll probably be scheduled for regular visits with a physical therapist. You and a friend or family member should discuss how to best manage your physical surroundings when you arrive home from the hospital. You'll need someone pretty much around the clock to begin with, and then, as you become better able to manage, you'll want someone to check in on you several times a day.

Part of that "checking in" is to perform tasks you can't do yourself, of course, but a great deal of it is emotional support: You're going to need someone to urge you to get up and about, to make yourself do things that you may feel too weak and exhausted even to contemplate.

WHERE ILLNESS LEADS

When you're sick, you feel awful. And when you feel awful, it's hard to get motivated to get better. Particularly if you are elderly and suffer from osteoporosis, you can become involved in a vicious cycle of "not doing."

Suppose you break your hip and go through a lengthy period of painful recovery and physical therapy. You are weaker when you are still healing and therefore may feel anxious about doing any movement that might cause more pain or—worst-case scenario—another fracture. So you stop walking down the driveway for the mail, you sit and watch television instead of going out to your bridge club meeting, and you restrict your activities and motions until you are virtually a prisoner to your disease. And you become more depressed as you feel that there is less and less that you can do for yourself.

Osteoporosis can cripple in more ways than the physical. Social isolation and isolation due to sensory defects are major contributors to what physicians call "failure to thrive." Not being able to see or hear well or losing the level of alertness that comes from social interaction can lead to apathy and an unwillingness to get better.

This is only a symptom of the larger problems of society. The loss of extended family, the strains of urban life, make it hard on all of us but particularly the elderly who often live alone with no close family and few friends. Sometimes their closest ally is their home health aide. If they don't happen to be suffering from an illness that needs immediate daily attention, and they don't require home care, they may not have anyone to talk to. And who will make all the various decisions that a bedridden woman, who can no longer perform her daily chores, let alone keep up with a good dietary and exercise program, may simply not feel up to making anymore? She may not even feel close enough to anyone who could make decisions for her if she became incapacitated.

WHAT TO DO TO KEEP ACTIVE AND INVOLVED

Get yourself or your parent a phone with one-touch dialing for 16 numbers and corral a group of people who are home at different times and ask if they will agree to respond if you need help.

Find a weekly activity that's convenient for you to attend, one that will involve you with others. Make sure there's someone who can transport you to and from this activity if need be. Rather than selecting a physical regimen where you'll undoubtedly have plenty of excuses if you're not feeling well, make this something you can do whether you're on your feet or temporarily off them. You may wish to join a book club, a quilting or crafts group, a musical society, or a bridge club.

Be sure there is one friend or family member who has keys to your house or apartment and who can come in an emergency on the spur of the moment.

If you are bedridden for any length of time, make sure

you have a doctor with a beeper—and put the number right on your night table. You should also consider a First Call for Help or Lifeline hookup on your telephone.

A GROUP ACTIVITY

There are those who say that "adult communities" are an aberration of modern culture. Why should we isolate those who happen to be out of the work force, their children grown, their concerns considerably different from those of younger people?

But there is an upside to living with others who share your developmental stage in life. People understand. People want to do—or not do—the same things. And often, they want to do these things together.

You don't have to live in a communal setting to share common interests with people your age, but if you don't drive or can't for health reasons and the supermarket and drugstore don't deliver, it's useful to have others around who can help.

CAN YOU AFFORD TO GET OLD?

The social and emotional costs of osteoporosis in an older population are staggering. Imagine a woman of 91 breaking a hip. She lives alone, since her husband died ten years ago, and has no family close enough to care for her, since her two daughters moved across the country for career opportunities. She must therefore be placed in a short-term convalescent home. Medicare will cover the first 20 days of her stay and then partially cover days 21 to

100. But her hip isn't healing, and she needs long-term care.

The typical stay for an elderly person in a nursing home is 30 months, at a cost of about $5,000 or $6,000 a month. If she opts for home care, with a nurse coming in to care for her, the cost may be half that of a nursing home, but there are many other considerations, such as shopping and cooking and possible glitches in nurses' changing shifts.

Medicare doesn't cover long-term custodial care, and you only qualify for Medicaid if you are over 65 and impoverished. This cuts down or eliminates the options for many.

As a nation, we are growing older. By the year 2016, there will be more postmenopausal women in America than women of reproductive age. By the year 2040, those who are 65 and over will make up 22 percent of the population; those over 85 will make up 5 percent.

We owe it to ourselves to make absolutely certain that we never need to depend on being rich enough to be elderly and have osteoporosis. We owe it to our parents to encourage them to stay healthy, to eat right, to exercise, to medicate themselves properly, and to have regular physical checkups. By keeping mind and body intact for many decades to come, we can give ourselves the gift of active longevity.

NINE

SPECIAL CASES— OSTEOPOROSIS IN MEN AND YOUNG PEOPLE

Although most cases of osteoporosis result from either hormonal loss at menopause or the aging process, there are secondary causes of this disease. In this chapter, we will explore the various reasons that young men, young women who go through early menopause, people who have been immobilized for long periods of time, and those on specific medications might develop osteoporosis.

OSTEOPOROSIS IN YOUNG MEN

Only 20 percent of all osteoporosis patients in the United States are male, and about half of those suffer the disease as a complication of *hypogonadism*. This condition occurs when a man's output of the hormone testosterone is insufficient to keep the bone remodeling process active and balanced.

Men may develop hypogonadism because of a pituitary

tumor, testicular atrophy, or some other endocrine malfunction. Hypogonadism can be treated with biweekly intramuscular injections of testosterone in an oil-based suspension.

In men, the hormone testosterone, produced by the adrenal glands and the testes, serves the same purpose that estrogen fills in women. It is responsible for the development of secondary sex characteristics like body hair, muscular development, and the deepening of the voice. Men need testosterone to be fully functional sexually—to achieve erection and produce semen in the testes. It also affects many metabolic activities, such as bone remodeling. Because a man's testosterone level remains relatively high throughout life, men are generally at lower risk for osteoporosis until they become elderly and the aging process takes its toll on bone mass and density.

The other causes of male osteoporosis are life-style factors: Heavy alcohol use, tobacco use, or being extremely thin puts men at much higher risk for this disease. Although it's not clear why alcohol affects bone turnover, a few clues have been uncovered. Alcohol seems to have a direct and toxic effect on bone cells. In addition, the chemical ethanol, which appears in high concentrations in liquor, reduces testosterone levels. (This is one reason why drinking before sex may heighten desire but lower performance.) Cirrhosis of the liver interferes with proper production of liver enzymes—which play an important role in calcium absorption. The bones of alcoholics that have been examined during an autopsy are considerably thinner than the bones of nonalcoholics.

Smoking is exceptionally detrimental to bone (in both men and women) because it inhibits proper oxygenization of the blood. Since the capillaries are not receiving an adequate blood supply, the bone tissue is not being sufficiently fed. Smokers also have up to 25 percent more disk degeneration than nonsmokers, which means that they have even less cushioning between their vertebrae.

The third factor, thinness, is also similar in men and women. Obese men tend to have more fat cells, which convert testosterone to estradiol (endogenous estrogen). And estrogen is of course beneficial to bone remodeling. Another important protective element connected with obesity is weight-bearing exercise—a heavy person puts more stress on the skeleton than a thin person, just moving around in the course of daily life.

The more risk factors a man has, the more likely he is to develop the disease. If he only drinks or only smokes, he is safer from osteoporosis than if he's thin and both smokes and drinks. And the older he is, the more risk involved, since age itself is a risk factor for osteoporosis.

SURGICAL MENOPAUSE

Women who have had their ovaries surgically removed because of disease are at high risk for developing osteoporosis.

If you no longer have ovaries, which produce estrogen and progesterone, you will immediately lose the protective effect of hormonal stimulation on your bones. Women who undergo a natural menopause lose this function gradually, over the course of years. But when your bones are robbed of all estrogen-progesterone protection at a time in your life where bone turnover is faster anyway, rapid bone loss becomes a serious problem.

If you have a diseased reproductive system, this operation must be performed in order to save you from life-threatening illness. It may also be performed as a preventive measure, to forestall the further growth of estrogen-related disease. If all the reproductive organs—your uterus, cervix, fallopian tubes, and ovaries—are excised, this is known as a *total abdominal hysterectomy and bilateral salpingo-oophorectomy (TAHBSO).* If only the ovaries are removed, it is known as an *oophorectomy* or *ovariectomy.*

This procedure is considerably more radical than a *hysterectomy,* where only the uterus and cervix are removed. If you have a condition that proliferates under the influence of estrogen, a hysterectomy will not be sufficient to treat it.

Severe (stage IV) *endometriosis* is one reason you might have to have your ovaries removed, but the most common reason is *estrogen-dependent cancer,* of which *ovarian cancer* is one type. The incidence of this cancer is very rare—only one in every seventy women will develop ovarian cancer during her lifetime. This accounts for only four percent of all cancers. Generally, it strikes women over age 50 when most are past the discomforts of hot flashes and other menopausal problems. But if there is evidence that the ovaries are diseased or irrevocably damaged, they should be removed.

Most physicians will urge their oophorectomized patients to take estrogen immediately following surgery unless they have had an estrogen-dependent cancer, in which case, calcitonin would be recommended. If you have no uterus, you will only need to take estrogen. You won't have to counter its effects with progesterone because you won't have an endometrial lining that might overgrow, putting you at risk for endometrial cancer. This means that, in addition to protecting your bones, you will be in better cardiac condition as well. An ERT regimen is twice as effective as an HRT regimen in reducing the risk of death from coronary artery disease.

Naturally, in addition to taking estrogen or calcitonin after oophorectomy, it is also necessary to maintain a good diet and exercise program and take calcium supplementation (1,200 to 1,500 mg daily).

If you have this operation when you are 25 or 30 years old and develop osteoporosis, you have that many more years ahead of you when you might be in serious danger of fracture every time you sneeze or bend over. It might become difficult or impossible for you to do any weight-bearing exercise, which would further increase your bone loss. The idea of being deformed by a hump due to repeated vertebral compression fractures, or worse, being bedridden with a hip fracture at such a young age, would be tragic because it would so drastically affect the quality of the rest of your many years to come. For this reason, preventive care and proper medication are absolutely essential.

OTHER LOSS OF OVARIAN FUNCTION

Young women athletes may also stop having periods. When we talk about the problems of athletes, we're not discussing average exercisers who follow a daily weight-bearing program, essential for adequate bone turnover. The kind of exercise that stops ovarian function is a demanding and rigorous type of training that uses up the body's metabolic and energy stores.

Women with eating disorders such as anorexia and bulimia may also lose ovarian function. If being thin is detrimental to bone, then being emaciated from self-imposed starvation is clearly worse. Anorexics and bulimics are depriving the growing body of much needed nutrients. Chronic dietary deficiencies in calcium and protein as well as many vitamins may lead to decreased bone mass.

In a severe state of stress, the body begins to shut down systems that are not absolutely essential, and the reproductive system is one of the first to stop functioning. When the hypothalamus and pituitary cannot hormonally stimulate the ovaries to mature eggs for ovulation, no estrogen or progesterone is produced. As we discussed in Chapter 7, these hormones are enormously influential in the body's ability to retain calcium in the bones.

A loss of ovarian function in younger women is quite serious. As with women who have been oophorectomized during their reproductive years, those who lose ovarian function have that many more decades to experience bone loss. And losing estrogen from athletic training or eating disorders means that the body's estrogen supply drops sharply in a short period of time, as opposed to tapering off over a period of years, as is the case with a natural menopause.

Interestingly enough, a small amount of weight gain—as little as five pounds—and a small cutback in athletic training may be sufficient to allow the body to resume menses. But women who lose ovarian function because of dietary or exercise disorders will always have a lower bone density than those who have had regular periods. Even after their systems get back on track, they can never recoup the amount of bone lost during the peak bone-growth years.

GLUCOCORTICOID THERAPY

Osteoporosis is a real threat to anyone on long-term glucocorticoid therapy. At least 50 percent of patients who take these medications contract the disease.

Glucocorticoids are a class of drug that treat chronic inflammatory diseases such as asthma, arthritis, rheumatic disease, and inflammatory bowel disease. They also suppress the immune system. The family of drugs—which includes prednisone, hydrocortisone, cortisone, methylprednisolone, and betamethasone, to name a few—consists of adrenal cortical hormones that affect protein and carbohydrate metabolism. Because they treat chronic diseases, they require long-term use. When the disease strikes in childhood, the way asthma often does, you must take the medication throughout your life.

Unfortunately, glucocorticoids' effect on bone remodeling is devastating—the drugs decrease calcium absorption from the intestine. They decrease vitamin D metabolism and increase urinary calcium excretion. They block the repair mechanism in bone so that bone formation slows to 70 percent of its former rate and bone resorption is increased. The drugs also affect PTH levels, prostaglandin, and growth hormone production. Dosages of 7.5 mg or more daily of prednisone have been shown to cause significant trabecular bone loss, and even cortical bone becomes more fragile over time.

The younger you are, the more quickly you lose bone on this type of medication. You're not even protected if you're in a traditionally low-risk category for osteoporosis: Blacks and men lose bone just as rapidly as white women. Postmenopausal women still lose the most bone, since they have also lost their protective estrogens.

It's essential that you discuss your osteoporosis profile

with your doctor if you are on these medications. You will naturally want to be on as low a dosage of your drug as possible, and if you can use a form of the drug that isn't systemic—a topical ointment, a nasal spray, or inhaler that doesn't have to work through your bloodstream—your bones may incur less damage. The particular glucocorticoid known as Deflazacort may have the least inhibitory effect on calcium absorption.

You'll need to supplement your diet with at least 400 IU of vitamin D and 1,000 to 1,500 mg of calcium daily, depending on your age. A well-balanced diet and exercise program is vital (see Chapter 5). If your densitometry reading indicates that you have already lost a good deal of your bone mass, you will want to consider one of the medical treatments discussed in Chapter 7 such as HRT or calcitonin.

One hopeful note is that glucocorticoid-induced osteoporosis appears to be partly reversible. This means that if your doctor decides your condition has improved measurably and you are able to discontinue or greatly reduce your drug use, you will be able to begin recouping some of your bone loss.

IMMOBILIZATION

If you survive a terrible car crash and end up in traction, your neck and most of your limbs broken, it's going to be a long time before your body can move at all—let alone effectively enough to prevent bone loss.

Bone mass declines when the body is not mechanically stressed. If you are forced to lie in bed for six months, you may lose 30 to 40 percent of your bone mass and density —just 36 weeks of immobilization is equivalent to ten years of aging on the skeleton. If you have ever broken a leg, and had to wear a hard cast for several weeks, you know what condition that leg is in when it's finally released from its prison. The muscles have shrunk, the skin texture is puckered, its color is pasty, and the connective tissues aren't flexible at all. If you measure the circumference of both legs, you'll find that the immobilized one is significantly smaller.

Remember that during any healing process the normal activity of cells is redirected toward the exceptional duty of rebuilding something that's been torn apart. This means that the osteoclasts, osteoblasts, and macrophages have to work double time for repair, and regular maintenance of the surrounding tissue goes by the board. The new bone that's been created won't be as strong as the old bone for quite a while. And if you are past 35, you will never regain all the mass lost, even if you're on a regimen of hormone replacement and calcium supplementation.

What happens during a period of immobilization is that the osteoclasts—the cells that resorb old bone—increase their activity. But with no mechanical stress to stimulate bone formation, the osteoblasts slow down or even cease functioning. In rats, it's been shown that the increase in bone resorption can be inhibited by giving them NSAIDs (nonsteroidal antiinflammatory drugs), like ibuprofen, possibly because these medications block prostaglandin synthesis (see Chapter 1 about the role of prostaglandins in osteoporosis). Other ways to slow bone resorption in immobile patients involve the use of calcitonin or a bisphosphonate.

There is no doubt that a program of physical therapy and subsequent daily weight-bearing exercise will be essential in the healing process. Calcitonin and bisphosphonates are two modalities of treatment to move the process along. Just how fast you go and how much bone mass, density, and physical mobility you regain depend on dozens of factors—not the least of which is your determination and sheer will.

JUVENILE OSTEOPOROSIS

This condition is very rare and generally occurs in children before the age of puberty. It might first be diagnosed when the child fractures a bone without any noticeable accident causing it. These children have very low bone mass and a negative calcium balance in their blood. No one knows exactly what causes this condition, although an abnormality in the immune system or a reduced production of growth hormone among other hormones might be partly responsible. Happily, most children with this disease undergo a spontaneous remission by puberty.

MEDICAL CONDITIONS PREDISPOSING YOU TO OSTEOPOROSIS

If you suffer from any of the following conditions or have undergone any of the following treatments, you should discuss your risk for osteoporosis with your physician and get on a good preventive care program:

Malabsorption syndromes

Rheumatoid arthritis

Chronic renal failure

Chronic liver disease

Hyperthyroidism

Cushing's disease

Hypogonadism/premature menopause

Primary hyperparathyroidism

Amenorrhea

Idiopathic hypercalciuria

Diabetes mellitus (type I)

TREATMENTS PREDISPOSING YOU TO OSTEOPOROSIS

Gastrectomy

Corticosteroid therapy (for asthma, rheumatic disease, inflammatory bowel disease)

Anticonvulsants

Excessive thyroid hormone replacement

Loop diuretics

Long-term tetracycline use

Prolonged heparin therapy (anticoagulant)

Radiation therapy to the spine

TEN

ADJUNCT TREATMENTS, PHYSICAL AND EMOTIONAL

Clearly, osteoporosis is a disease that must be treated with preventive care and excellent medical supervision. But many mysteries remain about the mechanisms of the disease, and medical science cannot at this time claim that any one treatment or combination of treatments will be suitable for every patient. For this reason, many people choose to expand their possibilities by using other modalities of treatment that may accompany medication, diet, exercise, and life-style precautions—*but only when authorized by a medical doctor.*

These therapies, used in *addition to traditional treatments,* attempt to ease pain and reduce stress in natural ways. They include physical therapy, different pain management techniques, movement management to strengthen the body's musculoskeletal system, psychological counseling, and alternative dietary/mineral supplementation approaches.

Many physicians acknowledge that a combination of approaches to dealing with the various facets of osteoporosis, if complementary, can afford a well-rounded treatment regimen. If you are interested in exploring any of these therapies, you must first discuss them thoroughly with your doctor and *use them only in conjunction* with your regular medical treatment. For some, like physical therapy, you must have a prescription from your doctor for the therapist to be able to treat you.

PHYSICAL THERAPY

Physical therapy is a type of treatment that attempts to relieve pain and rehabilitate the patient who is not physically functional because of disease processes or injuries that have affected movement. The treatment combines pain management, patient education, and gentle, beneficial exercise, completely personalized and adapted to the specific needs of each patient.

A physical therapist must be licensed by the state in which he or she works and can practice only with a doctor's prescription. This means that the doctor must work closely with the patient and therapist to collaborate on the best treatment that will take effect in the shortest period of time. The goal, of course, is to reduce or eliminate pain and to get the patient mobile again.

Reducing the Pain

When being treated by physical therapists for pain associated with osteoporosis, their collaboration is particularly important since this disease takes so many forms. A person who is at high risk but hasn't yet sustained a fracture may suddenly experience a period of rapid bone turnover, and the mildest exercise may be dangerous. Another person who has been diagnosed with osteoporosis and has had several hairline fractures may be a slow bone loser and may be able to perform all the therapist's exercises with less threat of compromising her health.

A good therapist will, with the doctor, evaluate your situation and come up with an appropriate plan of treatment.

The first line of attack for the therapist is to relieve or lessen the pain you are experiencing due to your osteoporosis. He or she must be told by your physician whether you are experiencing pain caused by static or dynamic forces. Dynamic pain results when you've performed a particular motion too vigorously, and your bone has fractured because of its brittle condition. Static pain is generally located in the lower part of the middle back or the upper part of the lower back where the curvature of the arc of your spine changes. This kind of pain occurs when a sustained load of weight proves too much for the weakened bone structure and a vertebra cracks under the pressure. This is known as a *compression fracture*.

The therapist may treat acute pain with a session using a transcutaneous electrical nerve stimulation (TENS) machine, especially in situations where muscle spasms around the fracture site have immobilized the spine in place. Pain is a protective mechanism: When the muscles beside the affected vertebrae contract, the spine is unable to move and injure itself further. The gentle electrical stimulation of the TENS unit massages the muscles to release their spasm so that the therapist can begin exercising the affected area. (See pages 154–155 for an explanation of how TENS works on pain.) Depending on the affected area and the amount of pain, the therapist will find a setting on the machine where the patient experiences a comfortable tingling and will leave it in place for 10 to 30 minutes.

If you are in a lot of pain, the therapist may prescribe a corset to reduce the mobility of your back. Wearing one of these, particularly on long car rides where the body is jostled by bumps and potholes, increases stability and makes certain your spine won't be compromised by excessive motion.

Patient Education

The next goal of the physical therapist is to teach you how to perform actions and hold positions—standing, sitting, lying down—you have taken for granted for years. Posture education is one of the most important lessons you can learn when you have osteoporosis or are at risk for it. The therapist will demonstrate that your spine is formed in a double-*S* curve. The spine is brilliantly designed to act like a shock absorber. Each vertebra is made so that the spine will have equal stress throughout its length when you sit and stand in the correct posture. If you slouch, you constantly strain your lower back. That, on top of low bone density, can cause fracture.

Look at the example of the spine maintaining good posture on the facing page. There is *lordosis* (inward arch) in the cervical or neck area; then a reverse curve, *kyphosis* (outward arch), in the thoracic or upper back; and then another *lordosis* in the lumbar or lower back area.

If you have had bad posture your entire life, you probably get tired easily when you stand or sit. *Bad posture* is either slouching forward, rounding the shoulders and chest and therefore throwing the lower back out of alignment, or overarching and swaybacked, thrusting the chest

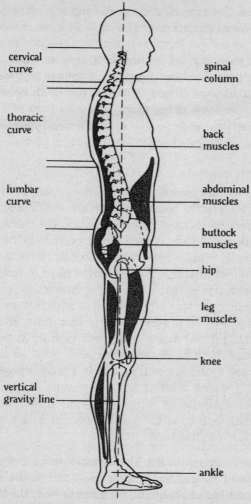

Normal spine, good posture.

cervical curve

spinal column

thoracic curve

back muscles

lumbar curve

abdominal muscles

buttock muscles

hip

leg muscles

knee

vertical gravity line

ankle

A healthy back has three natural curves. Good posture means keeping these three curves in balanced alignment. To do so, your muscles and joints must be strong and flexible.

and rear out (the classic "army sergeant" stance). *Good posture* maintains a normal arch in all three curves of the spine.

The therapist will demonstrate how to stand and sit properly. At first, the change in alignment will feel completely awkward to you, but after two or three weeks of practice in front of the therapist and in front of a mirror at home, your muscles will strengthen and your body will start to adapt and change so that this new posture will feel normal.

How to hold your back. Your back is stronger when you sit correctly because forces are distributed to the spine in its most natural position. The therapist will ask you to sit in your usual posture as he or she gently presses against one shoulder, then the other. You will find that it takes a lot of effort to resist being pushed over. You'll feel all the muscles in your chest and upper arm area fighting to maintain an upright posture. Now you'll try it, this time sitting up straight and maintaining your lordosis in the lower back. With hardly any effort at all, with no strain on your muscles, you'll be able to remain upright, feeling strong. Cutting out bad posture is like cutting out cigarettes: It seems impossible at first, but if you stick with it, within a few weeks you'll have formed a new, positive habit.

How to sit supported. The therapist will show you how to sit in a chair, using a towel roll at the small of your back to maintain the lordosis. (Let the therapist customize a towel roll for your body. Generally, you'll want something about a foot long and as wide around as a salami. It should fit comfortably into the

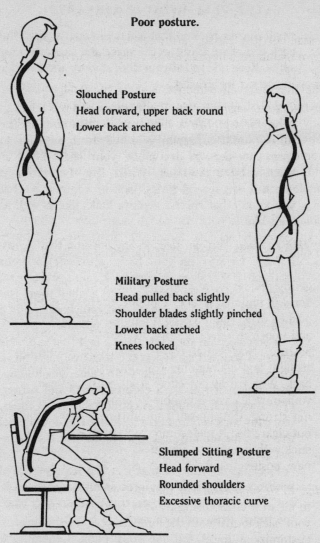

Poor posture.

Slouched Posture
Head forward, upper back round
Lower back arched

Military Posture
Head pulled back slightly
Shoulder blades slightly pinched
Lower back arched
Knees locked

Slumped Sitting Posture
Head forward
Rounded shoulders
Excessive thoracic curve

Poor posture distorts the body's proper vertical alignment and the back's natural curves.

small of your back so that when you lean against the back of a chair, it fills in the space and supports your spine. Keep one roll at your desk at work and another in the car for driving.)

How to sit unsupported. The therapist will teach you to bend forward like a hinge, while maintaining the lumbar lordosis, keeping your body from your hips to your shoulders in one piece, your chest lifted as though by a fishhook. When the therapist has checked you several times, look in a mirror so that you know what correct posture looks like as well as feels like.

How to sleep. You can sleep in any position that's comfortable for you: on your back, your side, or your stomach. If you sleep on your back, you should lie on a firm but not rigid mattress with a small towel roll under the small of your back and your knees up at a 45-degree angle, propped up with pillows.

If you sleep on your side, take a belt that is a little large on you and construct the towel roll around it. Then put the belt on, and your spine will be supported even if you are a chronic tosser and turner. (The towel roll should feel comfortable at all times, like your back is filling up a little bit. If it doesn't feel this way, it's too big, and you should have the therapist check it.)

Sleeping on your stomach is the least preferred position. It does give you lordosis in the lower back, but if you have osteoporosis, this position may place too much strain on your neck.

Your Monitored Exercise Program

The next step of physical therapy is to guide the patient, if she is able, through some gentle exercises. (Please note that any exercises you attempt must be prescribed by your doctor or physical therapist for your particular condition.)

Be very careful with every exercise you attempt. For someone at risk for osteoporosis, activities that look absolutely nonthreatening can cause fracture. All exercises should be exceptionally gentle, mostly static, and dynamic exercises must be low-key and slow. If you can avoid weight bearing, for example, by doing the exercises in water, this will take stress off the bone.

It is enormously important—whether you have already sustained fractures or are at high risk for osteoporosis—to strengthen those muscles you hardly ever use but that play a vital part in the functioning of your spine. When you are trained to work your *paravertebral* muscles surrounding the vertebral column, you relieve stress on the bones and stretch the ligaments and tendons that can be painful if you are healing from a fracture or injury.

A particularly effective static exercise to strengthen this area is performed as you lie on a table. The therapist has you lift an arm or clasp both hands and raise them as the therapist gives gentle resistance to the arm or arms. For the arm not to move, it must be braced by another part of the body, which in this case is the trunk. In order to keep the trunk stable, you must use your abdominal muscles; by using your abdominal muscles, you stabilize the middle and lower back. This kinetic chain from the arm through the spine offers a perfect lesson in body mechanics: By gently stressing one area, all the connected areas also benefit.

Another good static exercise is a gentle pelvic tilt,

where the patient lies on her back with her feet flat on the table, her knees at a 45-degree angle. The therapist shows her how to contract her abdominal muscles as she tucks her hips under her, then releases the muscles as she restores the lordosis to her lower back.

The therapist will of course monitor your own exercise program if you are already on one. Walking is generally recommended, if you are able. Weight training, with very light weights to start, is also beneficial. You should use only one- or two-pound weights; it's much better for you to lift small weights 20 times than heavy weights 10 times, because you can work in more movement with less strain.

If your condition makes it impossible for you to walk or lift, the therapist will probably recommend swimming. Before you have osteoporosis, you want to stress your bones with weight-bearing exercise. But after you have it, this may be too much for you. In this case, swimming is the best choice because it uses almost all the muscles in the body.

Your prescription for physical therapy will depend entirely on your condition. If you have only hairline fractures and not much pain, the therapist will see you two or three times and concentrate on an education and exercise program and work on posture and movement changes that will prevent further fractures in the future. If you have severe osteoporosis and a great deal of pain, the main job of the therapist will be to relieve the secondary symptoms like muscle spasms and pain so you can function again. This treatment, which may last for a couple of months, is successful when the pain is relieved or greatly lessened.

Relearning Activities You Enjoy

A physical therapist can be most helpful in giving you instruction in safer ways to do physical things you've always enjoyed.

Gardening. If you enjoy getting down on your hands and knees and pulling weeds, you must learn to do this without stressing your back. Get a plastic or wooden milk box and turn it on end. Then lean your chest on the box as you pull weeds or dig.

Golf. A good golf swing usually involves torquing your back—that is, turning your torso backward while leaving your legs and hips facing front. A physical therapist can show you how to move so that you turn something like an agitator in a washing machine—keeping the entire spinal column in one piece as you turn—and use your wrists more effectively to hit the ball.

Sexual activity. Certain physical therapists, urologists, and gynecologists are giving a new meaning to the words "safer sex." Working with the patient's physical limitations, the instructor can demonstrate different positions and angles that will be more comfortable and less hazardous on the spinal column and hips.

It's the job of a good therapist to convey the importance of not overdoing and of performing activities in harmony with proper body mechanics. He or she can't restore all your bone tissue any more than diet and exercise can, but can work with you to strengthen the bone you have and alert you to ways in which to protect yourself.

Finding a Qualified Physical Therapist

You will be recommended to a therapist by your physician. Many licensed physical therapists belong to the American Physical Therapy Association (APTA). (See Chapter 11.)

PAIN MANAGEMENT

Pain is the undesirable but fairly constant companion of many who suffer from osteoporosis, particularly those who have sustained many vertebral compression fractures. You don't have to tolerate excruciating agony, but you don't have to medicate it away either. It is better to use analgesics and narcotics sparingly if at all because they will interfere with your nutritional and vitamin/mineral supplementation program. In addition, drugs may affect your balance and perception, making falls more likely. It is important for you to take the time and effort to learn new ways to coordinate your mind and body to regulate pain.

Many doctors feel that if you know what to do when you feel physically overwhelmed by your symptoms, you can reduce stress and actually reduce the pain. Some traditional physicians use these methods along with conventional therapies.

Acupuncture

Acupuncture is a complex system of Eastern medicine, commonly used for pain relief, medical treatment, and analgesia in Asia, based on energetics rather than biochemistry. Acupuncturists use superfine, disposable, stainless-steel needles that are manually twirled or stimulated with electrical current on particular points in the body. The acupuncture needles access the body's natural energy. About 500 of these points, located along 12 so-called meridians, have been identified in the body, although most acupuncturists use only about 150 in treatment.

Many patients who try acupuncture for pain relief report a high degree of success. How can we explain this from a Western perspective? It's possible that the twirling needles trigger a release of endogenous opiates, which can relieve pain. Although Western medicine has made great progress in exploring the electrical potential of the body, it is still not clear why acupuncture is so effective. But millions of people who've tried it swear that it is.

If you are treated by an acupuncturist for pain relief in your spine, hip, or arm, the needles will be inserted along the particular meridian that connects points that lead to the source of the pain. The needles' stimulation will rush energy from a point on the hand or foot, for example, along the whole meridian through the affected organ and will move any blockage that might exist along this path. The way the needle is inserted can make the energy in an organ stronger or pull excess energy out.

Many Western medical doctors have been trained in the use of acupuncture for pain relief, using needle stimulation to block the passage of the pain from nerve endings to the brain.

Finding a Qualified Acupuncturist For a referral to an acupuncturist or to a pain management center that uses acupuncture as part of its program, ask your doctor or contact a local university hospital or medical school. In many states, acupuncturists must be licensed to practice. If this is true in your state, you can ask your state medical board for their names.

It is essential that the acupuncturist you select always use completely sterile equipment, that is, needles that are used on you and you alone. This is to guard against the spread of both hepatitis and the human immune deficiency virus (HIV) that causes AIDS (acquired immune deficiency syndrome), both of which can be transmitted through shared needles.

Acupressure

The principles of acupressure are similar to those of acupuncture, but the practitioner uses directed finger-point stimulation to access the body's meridians. Many patients prefer acupressure to acupuncture because it is noninvasive.

Acupressure practitioners are on staff at pain clinics, or you may find one through a university hospital or medical school.

Transcutaneous Electrical Nerve Stimulation

In transcutaneous electrical nerve stimulation (TENS) treatment, a weak electrical current from a TENS machine is passed through electrodes held by foam pads on top of your skin near the site of your pain. There are two theories as to how TENS stimulation works. One is that the stimulation of the electrodes blocks pain impulses from the afflicted organs to the brain. This may cause the release of *endorphins,* natural opiates produced by the brain, into the blood and spinal fluid. Another theory is that the procedure shuts down the connection between the source of the pain and the pain-receiving center in the brain.

Many medical centers and university hospitals have TENS machines, as do specialized pain clinics. Generally, your doctor would give you a prescription to see a physical therapist, a physiatrist, or specialized pain clinic practitioner at a facility where such a machine can be used in conjunction with the rest of your therapy.

MOVEMENT MANAGEMENT: FLEXIBILITY AND BALANCE EXERCISE

Two types of movement that are particularly beneficial in retaining the natural flexibility of tendons and muscles and in establishing balance (physical and emotional) and strength have been practiced for thousands of years. They should only be considered as preventive care if your physician feels that you are not severely limited physically; they are not advisable for those with spinal or hip fractures.

Yoga

Yoga is a series of postures, or *asanas,* held for different periods of time while the student works on breathing deeply and completely into all parts of her body. According to Indian thought, *prana,* or "energy," is the power at the base of life. The practice of yoga keeps the *prana* in balance, which in turn keeps mind and body in balance.

Some postures involve the body in unusual contortions and are not recommended for patients with advanced osteoporosis. Those who are at risk but have not suffered any fractures should try these postures *only* under the supervision of an experienced teacher who has worked with osteoporosis patients and only after the easier postures have been mastered.

Tai Chi

Chinese monks in the sixth century A.D. adapted Indian *asanas* into different series of moving postures, so they could keep active. These yielding and attacking postures are performed in complete relaxation with no force but rather with *chi,* which like *prana,* means "energy."

The tai chi postures apply the principles of *yin* and *yang,* the complementary opposites inherent in all things —hard and soft, fast and slow, light and dark—which, in combination, balance each other.

As with any form of exercise, it is important to learn the right—relaxed—way to perform these movements so as to stress the body as little as possible. When the postures are learned under the supervision of a qualified teacher who understands body mechanics, the balance, strength, and flexibility of the entire body will improve dramatically over time.

PSYCHOLOGICAL COUNSELING

Patient education has made great inroads in the prevention and treatment of osteoporosis, but it simply can't alleviate the stress that comes with the disease. The isolation and complications of being physically limited can make a patient feel helpless and, consequently, limit her progress in treatment. If you feel hopeless about improving your condition, it's difficult to comply with a diet, exercise, and medication program.

Some osteoporosis clinics make sure every patient sees a psychiatric social worker in addition to a physician, a nutritionist, and a physical therapist. It's just as important to deal with the fears and expectations of each patient as it is to recommend additional calcium. A counselor can discuss coping strategies with a patient and her family that can help greatly in dealing with change.

Imagine, for example, how family dynamics can shift dramatically when the woman of the house is afflicted with osteoporosis and can't perform her normal duties. If she can't lift, she can't go to the grocery store alone and do the family shopping; if she's unable to make beds, scrub floors, and drive to the mall, someone else in the house—usually her husband—will have to assume her jobs. Suppose she earned a considerable salary, which would no longer be available to the family if she was disabled? What if she lives alone? Or is the primary caretaker for a young child? Osteoporosis can cause many lives to fall into disequilibrium.

It's vital for each patient and his or her family to have a thorough grasp of the emotional ramifications of the disease. A few sessions of counseling with a trained social worker can prevent permanent demoralization from occurring.

Another big help in the emotional spectrum is having a support group. If you suffer from osteoporosis, you often feel like you're the only person in the world going through this experience. Ask your physician or social worker if it's possible to get the names of other people in treatment so you can get together and talk about your condition. Studies at Duke University have found that groups of patients in treatment together help each other cope.

OTHER NUTRITIONAL APPROACHES

High Magnesium Diet

In order to keep bone tissue strong as we get older, as we've said before, a diet rich in certain vitamins and minerals is essential. But there is some controversy about the amounts of those elements we ingest and how they interact with endogenous hormones and enzymes.

Calcium supplementation has always been the first line of treatment for those at risk for or suffering from osteoporosis. But there is a small group of researchers and physicians who feel that magnesium is as important or conceivably more important in the intricate mechanism of this disease process.

Magnesium is involved in calcium metabolism. These two minerals work intimately together in the processes of bone remodeling. Magnesium is also influential in the way the body uses vitamin D and in maintaining bone integrity. Dietary magnesium can be found in millet, potatoes, corn, wheat, brown rice, barley, and lentils—whole foods that are not commonly part of the American diet. Most of the complex carbohydrates we purchase in the supermarket, like white rice and wheat cereal, have been highly processed. Processing strips these foods of a great deal of their magnesium content.

Physicians who feel that magnesium deficiency and malabsorption are responsible for osteoporosis recommend a supplement of 1,000 mg magnesium daily and only 500 mg calcium (the reverse of what is commonly recommended). Several small-scale studies of women also on hormone replacement therapy as well as the dietary magnesium program who tested at risk for fracture because of low bone density showed marked improvement in a year.

Evidently, the women in this study also felt healthier because of their well-rounded mainly vegetarian, magnesium-rich diet. And eating less animal protein meant that they were losing less calcium through their urine.

Larger-scale trials on older patients and patients who are only taking magnesium without estrogen replacement are currently under way.

Foods as Medicine

An innovative approach that goes back to the treatments of our forefathers who relied on folk medicine for their health is based on the pharmacological properties of food. No less an authority than the U.S. Department of Agriculture has been testing the benefits of eating certain foods to help cure certain illnesses.

For osteoporosis prevention and treatment, nutritionists who use foods as medicine recommend a mainly vegetarian, high-fiber diet:

• Whole grains

• Green leafy vegetables

• Seaweeds

• Fish protein (sardines, salmon)

• Alfalfa

- Kelp

- Dried fruits

This diet is exceptionally low in dairy and tries to eliminate processed foods entirely because they are high in phosphorus. Animal protein and fats are also prohibited because they are low in magnesium and animal protein is highly acidic. In order to balance the body, calcium is pulled from the bones back into the blood to neutralize it.

Some nutritionists use herbal mixes in addition to diet. A tea or tincture of oat-straw-horsetail is sometimes recommended, but it will not be effective if there's a lot of yeast in your diet. Yeast is high in phosphorus and deficient in calcium.

Nutritionists who believe that food has healing properties emphasize the fact that you cannot change the habits of a lifetime overnight and expect to cure a disease. A well-rounded approach to the body means that you can't start after menopause to make up for the dietary neglect of decades. The bones you could have at 90 depend in great part on the bones you helped build from 7 to 18. Rather than boosting one vitamin, mineral, or food group now, nutritionists counsel you to eliminate or cut down on processed foods, sugar, all fats except olive and canola oils, and red meat.

A COMBINATION OF HEALTHY APPROACHES

Osteoporosis management must be handled through a cooperative alliance between you and your physician. What you eat, how you move, and how you deal psychologically with pain or limited movement will all affect the way you will handle your later years. When you and your doctor are aware of all the adjunct treatments for this condition, your possibilities for an easier, more comfortable life are greatly increased.

ELEVEN

WHERE TO GO FOR HELP

If you have osteoporosis, you have a chronic disease. It will probably require careful management from your mid-life years onward. Though there have been enormous advances made in the study, diagnosis, and treatment of osteoporosis in the last ten years, there is no cure. This means that you, as an informed medical consumer, owe it to yourself to use every resource at your disposal to get as much help as you can.

A library in a good-sized city will be your first best source of research and information. Most university or hospital libraries also allow the public access to their books and medical research services, though some may charge a fee for use.

There are a variety of specialized organizations and many allied support and self-help groups you can investigate.

NATIONAL ORGANIZATIONS

1. National Osteoporosis Foundation
   1150 17th Street NW, Suite 500

Washington, DC 20036-4603
1-800-223-9994

NOF is the main voluntary foundation for osteoporosis. It is an invaluable resource for medically sound information and program materials on the causes, prevention, and treatment of the disease. They have a research grant program, offer educational conferences for physicians, and run a yearly public-awareness campaign on osteoporosis. They also maintain a national osteoporosis information center staffed by a registered nurse. Their excellent booklet, "Boning Up On Osteoporosis," is available for $2, and they provide many specialized pamphlets on different subjects related to osteoporosis.

2. National Institute on Aging
   P.O. Box 8057
   Gaithersburg, MD 20898-8057
   (301) 495-3455

   A federally funded institute on all aspects of aging, including disease prevention.

3. National Institute of Arthritis, Musculoskeletal and Skin Diseases (NIAMS)
   A Division of the National Institutes of Health
   9000 Rockville Pike
   Building 31, Room 4C05
   Bethesda, MD 20892
   (301) 496-8188

   The leading government institute for research on osteoporosis and other musculoskeletal diseases. They publish pamphlets and a newsletter.

4. American College of Obstetricians and Gynecologists
   600 Maryland Avenue, SW
   Washington, DC 10014
   (202) 638-5577

   They can provide general information about osteoporosis and menopause.

5. The National Women's Health Network
   1325 G Street NW
   Washington, DC 20005
   (202) 347-1140

   They will send you a packet of resource materials on osteoporosis or any other disease or condition for a $5 fee.

6. American Geriatrics Society
   770 Lexington Avenue, Suite 300
   New York, NY 10021
   (212) 308-1414

   A medical organization composed of physicians concerned with research and the clinical treatment of the diseases of aging. They can refer you to specialists in your area.

7. Lifeline
   One Arsenal Marketplace
   Watertown, MA 02172
   (617) 923-4141
   1-800-LIFELINE

   A personal response system, available for a monthly rental fee of about $30 or $35. You wear a beeper that connects you via telephone linkup to responders (hospitals, police, ambulance, and personal emergency contacts).

8. National Association of Area Agencies on Aging
   1112 16th Street, NW
   Suite 100
   Washington, DC 20036
   1-800-243-4357

   This organization will give you a referral to agencies and organizations that deal with the issues of aging in your local area.

OSTEOPOROSIS CLINICS

In order to be treated for osteoporosis, you must know which specialist to consult. Most physicians who treat this condition fall into three categories: obstetrics and gynecology or endocrinology, orthopedics, and geriatrics. There are also several clinics specializing in osteoporosis and/or menopause around the country.

1. The Osteoporosis Center
   University of Connecticut Health Center
   Farmington, CT 06030
   (203) 679-1000

2. Regional Bone Center
   Helen Hayes Hospital, Route 9W
   West Haverstraw, NY 10993
   (914) 947-3000

3. Duke University Medical Center
   Department of Endocrinology, Metabolism and Nutrition
   Sarah W. Stedman Center for Nutritional Studies
   Durham, NC 27710
   (919) 684-5197

4. Mayo Clinic
   200 SW First Street
   Rochester, MN 55905
   (507) 284-2511

5. Emory Clinic
   Osteoporosis Evaluation
   1365 Clifton Road, NE
   Atlanta, GA 30322
   (404) 321-0111 or 248-3269

6. Jewish Hospital of St. Louis
   Osteoporosis Clinic
   4932 Forest Park
   St. Louis, MO 63110
   (314) 454-7156

7. Program in Osteoporosis and Bone Biology
   University of California at San Francisco
   1710 Scott Street, Third Floor
   San Francisco, CA 94115
   (415) 476-5549

8. Hospital for Special Surgery
   Osteoporosis Center
   535 East 70 Street

New York, NY 10021
(212) 606-1588

9. Center for Hard Tissue Research
   Department of Medicine, Creighton University
   601 North 30th Street
   Omaha, NE 68131
   (402) 280-4470

   Experimental research projects.

10. University of Pennsylvania School of Medicine
    Department of Orthopaedic Surgery
    425 Medical Education Building
    36th and Hamilton Walk
    Philadelphia, PA 19104-6081
    (215) 898-8653

    Experimental research projects.

NUTRITION

In order to rethink your nutrition for preventive osteoporosis care, you may wish to contact the following groups for their recommendations on diet.

1. American Dietetic Association
   216 West Jackson Boulevard
   Suite 800
   Chicago, IL 60606
   (312) 899-0040

   Will give referrals to dietitians in your area.

2. Center for Science in the Public Interest
   1501 16th Street, NW
   Washington, DC 20036
   (202) 332-9110

   Will provide resource information on high-calcium diets, including good food sources and supplementation.

PAIN MANAGEMENT

Because pain is a complex and difficult topic, you should do all you can to inform yourself about how the mechanisms of pain work and what you can do to alleviate it. The following groups may send you brochures on proven techniques, or they may provide referrals to pain management clinics near you.

1. American Society of Anesthesiologists
   515 Busse Parkway
   Park Ridge, IL 60068
   (312) 332-6360

2. American Pain Society
   P.O. Box 186
   Skokie, IL 60076
   (312) 475-1000

3. National Chronic Pain Outreach Association
   7979 Old Georgetown Road
   Suite 100
   Bethesda, MD 20814
   (301) 652-4948

4. National Institutes of Health
   Office of the Clinical Center for Communications
   9000 Rockville Pike
   Building 10, Room 1C255
   Bethesda, MD 20892
   (301) 496-2563

PHYSICAL THERAPY

Your physician will refer you to a physical therapist if he or she thinks you need one. Most belong to the association below, which also puts out some excellent pamphlets on posture, back care, and women's health.

American Physical Therapy Association
   1111 North Fairfax Street
   Alexandria, VA 22314
   1-800-999-APTA

WOMEN'S SUPPORT ORGANIZATIONS

One of the best resources for information and support for osteoporosis are the many groups founded and run by midlife and older women. Finding them will require a telephone directory and a little sleuth work. Try listings under "Social and Service Groups," "Women," and "Health."

1. HOT FLASH
   National Action Forum for Midlife and Older Women
   P.O. Box 816
   Stony Brook, NY 11790-0609

   Newsletter, $4 an issue or $25 a year.

2. A Friend Indeed
   P.O. Box 1710
   Champlain, NY 12919-1710

   Newsletter, $30 a year for ten issues.

3. Resources for Midlife and Older Women
   226 East 70 Street
   Suite 1C
   New York, NY 10021
   (212) 439-1913

   Medical and psychological referrals.

4. Women's Helpline (NOW, NYC Service Fund)
   15 West 18 Street, Ninth Floor
   New York, NY 10011
   (212) 989-7230

   Referrals to midlife women's groups and services.

5. Women's Health Center
   North Iowa Medical Center
   23 North Federal
   Mason City, IA 50401
   (515) 424-1100

   A doctor, nurse, counselor, and dietitian are on the
   premises for complete general health care.
   If a patient is at high risk for osteoporosis, they will
   refer her for more specialized care.

6. Midlife Women's Network Newsletter
   5129 Logan Avenue S.

Minneapolis, MN 55419-1019
(612) 925-0020

Indepth coverage of women's preventive healthcare issues.

LIBRARIES AND DATA BASES

Your public library can provide you with a great deal of information about osteoporosis. If you happen to live near a university with a medical center, or a Veterans Administration Hospital, you can probably gain access to up-to-date research through their libraries, which are generally open to the public.

1. Center for Medical Consumers/Health Care Library
   237 Thompson Street
   New York, NY 10012
   (212) 674-7105

   A wonderful resource for books and the latest articles in traditional and alternative medicine. They also publish a monthly newsletter called "Healthfacts," available by subscription.

2. The Health Resource
   Janice R. Guthrie
   209 Katherine Drive
   Conway, AR 72032
   (501) 329-5272

   Will provide a comprehensive report on traditional and nontraditional treatments. Each report costs $150.

3. Planetree Health Resource Center
   2040 Webster Street
   San Francisco, CA 94115
   (415) 923-3680

   Will provide up-to-date medical abstracts and articles on the latest research in the field for a range of fees.

4. World Research Foundation, California
   15300 Ventura Boulevard
   Suite 405
   Sherman Oaks, CA 91403
   (818) 907-5483

   This organization will do research for you on standard or alternative therapies currently in use for any disease or condition. For a fee, they offer either a computer search on conventional medical treatments or a library search on alternative therapies.

GLOSSARY

absorptiometry (single- and dual-photon and dual-energy X-ray): Special measurement techniques that can detect bone loss. In the first two techniques, the bone is scanned with one or two beams from radioactive isotopes. In the third, an X-ray source, rather than an isotope source, is used.

adrenal glands: Hormone-producing glands located just above the ovaries, one covering each kidney. In addition to supplying the body with additional estrogen and progesterone, as well as adrenaline, the adrenals secrete androgens (androstenedione and testosterone).

androgens: Hormones responsible for male sex characteristics, specifically, testosterone and androstenedione.

bisphosphonates: A family of nonsystemic drugs including etidronate, pamidronate, alendronate, and others that inhibit bone resorption by slowing down osteoclastic activity.

bone formation: Part of the process of remodeling that occurs throughout life. Formation is dependent on osteoblastic activity whereby bone-forming cells fill in cavities made when old bone is resorbed and lay down minerals that create new bone.

bone resorption: The other half of the process of bone remodeling. Resorption is dependent on osteoclastic activity whereby old bone is removed and its essential elements are returned to the bloodstream.

calcitonin: A hormone that lowers serum calcium, making more calcium available to the bones. This medication is generally prescribed for patients who do not choose to take estrogen or cannot because of certain contraindications.

calcium (calcium phosphate): A mineral carried by the blood that is the major element of bone tissue.

collagen: A protein that gives support and structure to connective tissue, such as skin, bones, and cartilage.

cortical bone: The smooth, firm external part of bone.

demineralization: The process of bone loss.

endocrine glands: Ductless glands that produce internal secretions––hormones—that circulate throughout the body through the blood or lymph systems. The principal endocrine glands are the pituitary, thyroid, parathyroid, adrenals, and gonads (ovaries and testes).

ERT (estrogen replacement therapy): Unopposed estrogen is prescribed for a patient without a uterus. May be given as oral therapy or as a transdermal patch.

estrogen: The hormone released by the ovaries as eggs mature. About 300 tissues of the body respond, directly or indirectly, to estrogen stimulation. After menopause, a woman's production of the hormone slows and eventually ceases, resulting in a variety of physical changes.

estrone: A watered-down form of estrogen. After menopause, the adrenals help the ovaries to secrete a male sex hormone, androstenedione, and convert it to estrone. Heavier women with more fat cells and therefore more estrone seem to have an additional protective factor against osteoporosis.

glucocorticoids: A class of adrenal cortical hormones used to treat chronic inflammatory diseases. These drugs decrease calcium absorption from the intestine and block repair mechanisms in bone. Long-term use is a risk factor for osteoporosis.

hormone: A substance secreted by a gland that travels through the bloodstream and, alone or in conjunction with other hormones, stimulates another part of the body to function by chemical action.

HRT (hormone replacement therapy): Therapy where estrogen is prescribed for the first 25 days of a woman's cycle and progesterone is added for days 12 to 25. Sometimes, continuous estrogen is given with two weeks of the progestin.

idiopathic osteoporosis: Osteoporosis that occurs for unknown reasons to people in low-risk categories such as children, young men, or premenopausal women.

kyphosis (dowager's hump): This deformity of the spine arises when compression fractures of the thoracic ribs change the curvature and alignment of the vertebrae.

lordosis: The natural S-curve of the spine at the neck (cervical) and below the waist (lumbar).

magnesium: A mineral involved in calcium metabolism.

matrix: Intercellular material in bone tissue made of protein threads (largely collagen). The matrix houses both organic (nerves and blood vessels) and inorganic (mineral) matter.

menopause: The event marked by a woman's last menstrual period. May be as early as 35 and as late as 60 but usually occurs between the ages of 47 and 52. A woman is said to have gone through the menopause when 12 months have passed without a period.

oophorectomy: A surgical procedure where the ovaries are removed.

osteoblast: A bone-forming cell.

osteoclast: A bone-resorbing cell.

osteocyte: A bone cell developed from the osteoblast. Its function seems to be making connections between other cells in the bone matrix.

osteomalacia (adult rickets): A condition where the bone itself is insufficiently mineralized, causing it to remain soft and not harden as in a normal growth process. This disorder occurs when the quality of the bone tissue declines, rather than the quantity—which is the case in osteoporosis.

osteopenia: Disease-, drug-, or malnutrition-related bone loss. This is a common complication of bone marrow tumors such as multiple myeloma.

osteoporosis ("porous bones"): A disease of bone loss that leaves bone excessively fragile and susceptible to fracture. Osteoporosis causes pain, disability, and even death.

ovary: One of two almond-shaped glands in the female body that contains eggs (ova). It produces the two hormones estrogen and progesterone.

parathyroid glands: Four small glands behind the thyroid gland responsible for raising blood calcium by producing parathyroid hormone (PTH).

progesterone: The hormone obtained from the corpus luteum (the body that remains after an egg has ovulated from its follicle). It is responsible for changes in the endometrial lining during the second half of a woman's cycle.

progestin (medroxyprogesterone acetate): A synthetic progesterone reconstructed in the laboratory for use in HRT.

QCT: Quantitative computed tomography: This type of CT

scan is used to measure bone mass and density of the lumbar spine.

sodium fluoride: A mineral often found in drinking water that makes teeth stronger and reduces cavities. It has been used experimentally as a treatment for osteoporosis, but the new bone formed during the treatment was found to fracture easily.

surgical menopause (see *oophorectomy*): The immediate cessation of estrogen and progesterone production that results after an oophorectomy (removal of the ovaries).

tamoxifen: An anti-estrogenic drug used in breast-cancer therapy. It has been recently shown to reduce bone resorption and stimulate bone formation.

TENS: Transcutaneous electrical nerve stimulation. A machine that assists the brain in blocking pain by passing a weak electrical current over the skin near the pain site.

testosterone: An androgen released by the testes. It's responsible for many masculine secondary sex characteristics and behaves for men's bones as estrogen does for women's, helping to retain calcium in the bones.

thyroid gland: A gland located in the base of the neck that produces hormones, including calcitonin, that regulate the metabolism of most of the body's cells, thereby stimulating growth and development.

trabecular bone: The honeycomblike, spongy, interior tissue of bone, threaded through with marrow, blood vessels, and capillaries.

transdermal patch: A round plastic patch impregnated with estrogen that is applied to the belly, back, or buttocks and changed twice weekly. In this method of dosage, the hormone released doesn't have to pass through the digestive system and be processed by the liver, a reason some physicians prefer it over the oral regimen.

vertebra: One of the 33 bones that make up the spinal column. Vertebrae are mostly trabecular bone, which makes them often prone to fracture in a patient with osteoporosis.

vertebral compression fracture: A break or crush in one of the vertebrae usually resulting from porous bone no longer able to support the weight of the spinal column. As more breaks occur over time, the vertebrae press on one another and often shift out of alignment.

INDEX

ABOUT THE AUTHOR

Judith Sachs, the daughter and granddaughter of physicians, was born in New York City. A health and medical writer and speaker, she is the author of *What Women Can Do About Chronic Endometriosis* and *What Women Should Know About Menopause* (Dell Medical Library Series), and is the co-author of *The Anxious Parent* with Dr. Michael Schwartzman (Simon & Schuster), *After the Fast,* with Dr. Phillip Sinaikin (Doubleday), and *Dr. Mollen's Anti-Aging Diet: The Breakthrough Program for Weight Loss and Longevity* with Dr. Art Mollen (NAL/Dutton). Judith Sachs conducts menopause and midlife workshops in central New Jersey, where she lives with her husband and daughter. She is currently working on a preventive health-care book that combines Eastern herbal and Western medical treatments.

Dell Medical Library